P9-ELW-424

IT HAPPENED IN
SOUTH CAROLINA

It Happened In Series

IT HAPPENED IN
SOUTH CAROLINA

*J. Michael McLaughlin
and Lee Davis Todman*

TWODOT®

GUILFORD, CONNECTICUT
HELENA, MONTANA
AN IMPRINT OF THE GLOBE PEQUOT PRESS

A · TWODOT® · BOOK

Copyright © 2004 by The Globe Pequot Press

All rights reserved. No part of this book may be reproduced or transmitted in any form by any means, electronic or mechanical, including photocopying and recording, or by any information storage and retrieval system, except as may be expressly permitted by the 1976 Copyright Act or by the publisher. Requests for permission should be made in writing to The Globe Pequot Press, P.O. Box 480, Guilford, Connecticut 06437.

TwoDot is a registered trademark of The Globe Pequot Press.

Library of Congress Cataloging-in-Publication Data
McLaughlin, J. Michael.
   It happened in South Carolina/ J. Michael McLaughlin and Lee Davis Todman.—1st ed.
      p. cm—(It happend in series)
   Includes bibliographical references and index.
   ISBN 0-7627-2452-8
      1. South Carolina—History—Anecdotes. I. Todman, Lee Davis. II. Title. III. Series

F269.6.M35 2003
975.7—dc22   2003061397

Manufactured in the United States of America
First Edition/First Printing

Contents

Acknowledgments

The joy of rediscovering history's little-known twists and turns is not a solitary pursuit. Thank goodness for that. While researching the stories for *It Happened in South Carolina,* we met and enjoyed the fellowship of many others—professional historians, librarians, lecturers, authors, supportive family and friends—all of whom helped make this work a pleasure.

First, we'd like to thank Harlan Greene for his early encouragement and helpful suggestions. His staff in the South Carolina Room at the Charleston County Library soon became accustomed to our frequent visits and endless requests for our archival gems from South Carolina's past.

The Charleston Library Society and The South Carolina Historical Society proved especially helpful retrieving rare resource material and publications that inspired us. The Preservation Society of Charleston was another treasure trove of information.

Friends of the Daniel Library at The Citadel, in its ongoing lecture series, was timely and enormously helpful in bringing us access to noted historians and experts on South Carolina history. In addition the Karpeles Manuscript Museum lecture series was enlightening about other aspects of the state's fascinating past.

Further afield the Rice Museum in Georgetown, South Carolina, helped bring into focus the vast impact of the state's rice culture. Visits to S.C. State Parks also proved illuminating.

The Avery Research Center for African-American History and Culture shed invaluable light into the darker aspects of the state's socioeconomic history.

We would like to thank our editor at The Globe Pequot Press, Erin Turner, for her patience and guidance through the yearlong writing process.

And finally we both thank our parents for instilling in us a love of history and its endless capacity to teach and entertain.

Preface

The writing of *It Happened in South Carolina* has been a dramatic reminder of one of the universal laws all writers of history eventually come to learn—that to *write* history (about South Carolina, in particular) is to *read* history. Almost without exception *someone* has undoubtedly written *something* about your subject *sometime* before. The well of history runs very deep.

Because so much has happened in the Palmetto State over the course of its checkered history, it seems the myriad of significant events and fascinating repercussions surrounding them have been described by writers of every stripe and persuasion for at least 300 years. So far. Their words fill whole libraries, and it's possible to reach back in time and see people and events from the past as clearly as we see South Carolinians today. It's also possible to find just as many contradictions and versions of "the truth" in the past as we find in the supposedly more complicated world of the Now.

The passions of historians being what they are, we acknowledge that there will be those who endorse one version of "the truth" over another. That's what makes reading history so interesting. If we've erred in this small volume, it was on the side of action—choosing the truth with greater action in an effort to ignite the imaginations of our readers, young and old. Once the fires of imagination are lit, then comes the illumination for insight and the eventual wisdom of perspective.

The stories we've chosen for *It Happened in South Carolina* lightly flit over the larger field of the state's history and sample nectar from only a few of the blossoms deeply rooted in this Southern American soil. It is hoped that readers of this book acquire a taste for this sweet (and sometimes sour) nectar and—like a hummingbird—return to this vast and colorful field again and again.

This we can promise: The blooms get more varied, the nectar's flavor gets richer, and the sense of discovery and wonder becomes more rewarding.

That's how it happened for us.

J. Michael McLaughlin
Lee Davis Todman
Fall 2003

A note about the name Charleston: Until the city of Charleston was incorporated in 1783, the spelling of the name varied widely. Throughout the book we've utilized the basic designations given in Robert Rosen's *A Short History of Charleston* for the evolving spelling of the name *Charleston* during the early history of the city:

Charles Towne: during the rule of the Lords Proprietors, 1670–1720

Charlestown: under the Royal Governors and during the Revolution, 1720–1783

Charleston: after the city was incorporated, 1783–present

Rebeckah and the Indian Squaw

· 1684 ·

Charles Towne Landing is where South Carolina's colonial story really begins. There, in the spring of 1670, two boatloads of English adventurers climbed off their ships at a site later known as Albemarle Point to establish the first permanent settlement in honor of King Charles II in the New World.

Daring as it was for these brave men and women to start life anew in a strange, untamed wilderness, it was a man's world. Women's lives were defined in large part by the work of their husbands or fathers, and that was that. Still, women accepted that colonial life was hard, and acknowledged that early death was a regular visitor to colonial homes. Without a man around to work and earn a wage, a woman could expect the effects of poverty and disease to come calling.

One such woman was Rebeckah Lee. She was a wife and a mother. Most of the other facts about her life have been lost. The exact date of her arrival in "Charles Towne," for example, is unclear. She wasn't listed among the 130 people aboard the first two ships, the frigate *Carolina* or the sloop *Albemarle*. Perhaps she arrived a few years later, when additional families from England and Barbados joined the original founders.

Rebeckah and her children were living in Charles Towne in the spring of 1684 (only fourteen years after the founding), when she apparently committed a crime.

By 1680, according to one account, the colony's population had grown to more than 1,000 souls. By then the colonists had abandoned Albemarle Point. For safety they had relocated to the city of Charleston's present site, on a nearby peninsula protected by two broad rivers. This site was far more defensible against pirates and the ever-present Spanish, who were aggressively colonizing Florida at the time. It was also safer in the event of attack from hostile Indians.

Therein lies the crux of Rebeckah's crime. She was accused of "fetching a drink [of rum] for an Indian Squaw." For that offense against the Crown, she was hauled before the Grand Council, a kind of court of law, where she made an eloquent plea for mercy. The fact that her plea actually survives is rare enough. But her words set down in the records of the court allow a few dim rays of enlightenment to shine into the dark picture of colonial women's lives.

Why would selling a drink to an Indian woman "to gett a penny," as Rebeckah explained it, be considered a punishable offense? How did making this small business exchange trespass against the safety of the colony? To answer that, it helps to analyze the community in which Rebeckah lived. Who were her neighbors and peers? Who would judge her so harshly?

Rebeckah lived in a world of tradesmen and planters who toiled in their houses or worked in fields outside the newly built town walls. Other Charles Towne citizens were more connected to the busy wharves where trade was coming and going with increasing frequency. Here thieves and rascals lurked about, and liquor flowed freely. Danger was omnipresent. Residents were safe enough by day outside the city walls, and if threatened, they could seek protection behind them by night. The sea, of course, was another risk. Ships fell prey to pirates and frequent storms, and many men sailed off, never to be seen or heard from again.

By her own account Rebeckah's husband was "away at sea." Her partner in life, her only acceptable source of income, was conspicuously absent. As far as she knew, her husband might be gone for months, even years. How could a woman in the early colony make a few coins to keep her children fed and clothed?

The rule of law in Rebeckah's time was not set down by the independent-minded rebels who evolved a century later on these shores. These were not yet "American patriots." The men, women, and children who settled Albemarle Point and moved on to the peninsula were Europeans who had little in common with our Founding Fathers yet to come. They were mostly strong-willed and loyal Englishmen, here to expand a decidedly English view of civilization, not create a new one. And women's rights would take another 300 years to evolve in our society.

The men of Charles Towne weren't deliberately cruel to women or even to the Indians they encountered; their focus was simply elsewhere. Their main concern was to meet the basic needs of survival during their first few years in a New World.

Almost immediately, food was a problem. Even though the sea and the land around them were abundant in fish and game, the first colonists might well have starved were it not for the generosity of the local Native Americans. Many small tribes of the Muskogean Indians populated the Charles Towne area. None of these tribes was large enough, or able enough, to organize much resistance to this English invasion. Despite occasional skirmishes the colonists found the local Indians generally friendly and willing to trade food and furs in exchange for beads, trinkets, and simple tools. It was the gift of meat and grain from the local Indians that staved off the terrible "want of victuals" during the first winter of 1670, but instead of offering gratitude to the Indians, the colonists took their assistance for granted. For the most part Indians were treated like untrustworthy children—rewarded with "trade" when good and punished severely when bad.

For a while at least, this arrangement between the colonists and the Indians remained peaceful. But as trade for food and furs became more important to the settlers and their developing economy, this once-friendly relationship quickly deteriorated. The Indians saw more and more of their lands being overtaken by slave-holding planters who kept moving deeper and deeper into the wilderness. At the same time the colonists resented the Indians who hunted on these same lands and made little distinction between taking game from the wild and killing the settler's precious breeding stock.

Friction soon developed, and much blood would be spilled as the years progressed. Ultimately, increasing abuse by inland traders and the introduction of intoxicants combined with the Europeans' infectious diseases took their deadly toll. Gradually the entire Indian population of the Carolina colony was tragically decimated.

In the bustling Charles Towne of Rebeckah's day, the sight of "Red Men" in and around the colony was still quite common, but only "professional traders" were supposed to do the talking. Civilian interaction with Indians was considered unwise; it might stir up unwanted trouble. In particular no woman had any business making deals with the Indians!

Presented with a fleeting chance to make a little money from an Indian woman, however, Rebeckah apparently found the temptation overwhelming. The ruling officer of the Royal Court surely looked down from his high bench of authority upon hapless Rebeckah as she approached the bench to answer for her crime. As she spoke, the court reporter's quill began to scratch the following entry on April 17, 1684:

To the honored County Court now sitting in Charles Towne The humble petition of Rebeckah Lee is:

That, whereas the petitioner unadvisedly have violated the law by fetching of Drink for an Indian Squaw though wholy ignorant of its being Contrary of Law, also being in a poor and low Condition, having nothing at present by what my husband having been gone long since to Sea. And the Indian tempting me with Sixpence for my pains,

*I was willing to gett a penny to relieve my Self and chil-
dren, and so fell into this offence.*

*Therefore the request of your poor petitioner is that this
honored Court would be pleased to Consider the
Condition of her your poor petitioner, and please pardon
this offense . . . she hopes and trusts it shall be a warning
to her forever hereafter, and this shall be a further obli-
gation to God as I am in duty bound to pray for your
health and happyness.*

As your petitioner,
Rebeckah Lee

When Rebeckah sold her "drink" to the nameless squaw,
the law she technically broke wasn't against doing business
with an Indian. The law forbidding the sale of rum to Indians
wasn't yet on the books. That would come later, but even after
it did, this prohibition had little impact on the trade that took
place between Indians and women like Rebeckah. Without
financial means of her own, she did whatever necessary in
order to survive. She was charged with breaking a law set
down even earlier—in 1672—prohibiting anyone in the colony
from selling liquor without a license.

Rebeckah's story must have been repeated a thousand
times as women became widows and faced the responsibilities
of raising fatherless children, an ocean away from their English
relatives and supportive friends. Whether or not Rebeckah was
granted the mercy of the Court is unrecorded, and it's unlikely
any point of view from the Indian's perspective was ever heard.
But Rebeckah's plea illuminates the distress of her life and her
time with stark reality. When seen through the contemporary
lens of present-day society, Rebeckah's plight reminds men and
women of all times, all places, and all positions of power . . .
to consider the important role women play in our interde-
pendent and multicultural world.

The Execution of Stede Bonnet

·1718·

The now constant threat of pirates marauding the Carolina coast had become intolerable, but London was indifferent to the colonists' woes. Governor Robert Johnson urgently requested assistance from England for a substantial force of trained soldiers and several ships to protect Charles Towne. No help was to come.

When the governor realized it was a waste of his time to beseech London further, he took matters into his own hands, turning to Col. William Rhett, a well-proven soldier-sailor, to hunt down and capture these despicable buccaneers.

In September 1718, with the support of angry and frustrated local merchants, Rhett equipped two ships, *Sea Nymph* and *Henry*, with 130 men and armament. He caught up with the infamous Capt. Stede Bonnet, refitting his sloop the *Royal James* in the Cape Fear River along coastal North Carolina, a popular hiding place for pirate ships due to the numerous inlets and the treachery of their many shoals.

On September 26 Rhett's ships entered the mouth of the dangerous inlet. Hurriedly completing repairs on *Royal James*, Bonnet started downriver for the open sea at dawn on the 27th. *Henry* intervened and was able to maneuver *Royal James* onto a shoal, but in the process both *Henry* and *Sea Nymph* ran aground as well. *Sea Nymph* ended up some distance away, but *Henry* was within firing range of the pirate ship. For hours the two ships fought fiercely with cannon and muskets while the tide continued to recede. Unfortunately for *Henry*, the shallow water level caused both vessels to heel over so that the angle of the tilted ships allowed *Royal James* the tactical advantage. The deck of *Henry* was exposed, and Bonnet seized the opportunity to pummel Rhett's crew, inflicting much damage and loss of life.

But as the tide turned and gradually righted the ships, Colonel Rhett's two ships floated first. They quickly moved into position and prepared to finish off Bonnet and his crew. Captain Bonnet, having earlier threatened his men to fight to the death, now opted for surrender.

Colonel Rhett brought thirty-five prisoners back to Charles Towne on October 3 and was hailed a hero. The pirate crew was imprisoned in the town bastion's guardhouse under close watch while waiting to stand trial. But Bonnet, known as "the Gentleman Pirate," and his sailing-master lieutenant, David Herriot, were placed under house arrest at the town marshal's home.

Days before the trials were to begin, the sentries stationed outside Marshal Partridge's house were bribed, enabling Bonnet and Herriot to escape, reportedly dressed in women's clothing. It is thought that several townspeople, who had known Bonnet (and perhaps had profited from dealings with him) did not want him to come to trial for fear that the testimony would be damaging to them by association. These sympathizers supplied a small boat, which Bonnet, Herriot, and two accomplices used to flee. Upon the news of their escape, Governor Johnson immediately posted a large reward for the recapture of these men "dead or alive."

Nothing in Stede Bonnet's upbringing would have predicted his life of crime on the high seas. Based on what little is known, his was a life most would have considered privileged. He was a well-educated man from a respected, aristocratic family. He served in the Royal Army of England, retiring as a major. After his military career, he grew wealthy as the owner of a large sugarcane plantation on the tropical island of Barbados, married, and fathered four children.

One day, Bonnet purchased a ship, hired a crew, and set sail out of Bridgetown Harbor for the high seas. No one seems to know why someone of his background and means would turn to a life of piracy.

One theory was that he suffered from a "disordered mind" or some type of dementia. Another was that boredom with a comfortable life—perhaps in present-day terms what would be called a "midlife crisis"—chafed him. Yet another popular legend proposed he was merely trying to escape from a nagging wife. Whatever the reason, this "gentleman" did attain a life of adventure and notoriety. In 1717 Captain Bonnet had very little knowledge of seamanship. He was considered unusual among buccaneers, because he had purchased his ten-gun sloop (instead of stealing it) and paid the members of his crew (instead of merely granting them a share of the booty). At first his seventy-man crew understandably mistrusted their inexperienced leader. He was soon to learn some invaluable lessons in the world of piracy, however.

Initially, Bonnet managed to capture and plunder a few merchant ships off the Virginia coast and near Charles Towne, but his crew was still not confident of their captain. Soon thereafter, Bonnet crossed paths with the infamous pirate Edward Teach, or "Blackbeard," only to become his prey when Blackbeard stole his ships and crew. During this time Bonnet was also witness to some of Blackbeard's legendary cruelty.

Eventually Blackbeard released Bonnet, and "the Gentleman Pirate" retook command of his ship, *Revenge*. It is believed that under Blackbeard's tutelage, Bonnet had learned some of the more cruel tricks of the trade. He adopted ruthless marooning, flogging, torturing, and slaying of both his crew and piracy victims. At first he sought revenge against Blackbeard but was unsuccessful in pursuing his captor. He refocused on preying on the lucrative trading vessels traveling between the east coast of North America and the Caribbean. This action met with much more success, and a series of captures not only filled his coffers but also assured the loyalty of his formerly contemptuous, if not mutinous, crew.

In May 1718 the residents of Charles Towne endured the pillaging of nine vessels and the seizure of many prominent passengers in their own harbor by Blackbeard's brigade. Boldly demanding medical supplies in exchange for hostages, Teach was able to force Governor Johnson to meet his demands. This incident, especially, left the colonists feeling extremely vulnerable, humiliated, and irate. By September, when Colonel Rhett had set out to capture Bonnet, the outrage had not abated. Bonnet's escape from the authorities in Charles Towne would not be tolerated.

Colonel Rhett raised a posse and once again set out to catch the elusive Bonnet. At the same time more pirate sloops showed up off the Carolina coast, and rumors were rampant that they were there for only one reason—to ransack Charles Towne. The governor, determined to strike back, called for an attack on the buccaneers. Four ships currently in port were commandeered for this purpose, outfitted with cannon, and disguised as merchant vessels. Demonstrating the vengeful mood of the residents of Charles Towne, 300 men eagerly volunteered for the crew.

As the latest threat to the town unfolded, the trial of Bonnet's crew convened in the Court of the Vice-Admiralty on October 28, with Chief Justice Nicholas Trott presiding. Several factors led to a speedy conviction of these men. Justice Trott was reputed to have great legal skill, if not a firm grip on what he referred to as "his" courts. The prosecutor, Richard Allein, Attorney General of Carolina, made the popular argument that the terrorizing of the colonists and the plundering of their commerce by bands of pirates must be brought to an end. Examples had to be made of these scoundrels if the inhabitants of Charles Towne were ever to feel safe and enjoy their burgeoning prosperity. The crew was even left without counsel, as was customary at the time; no attorney was present to assist in their defense. They entered a plea of "not guilty" on the grounds that they had been forced into a life of piracy by their captain. Justice Trott turned a deaf ear to this plea by pontificating and denouncing them all. Twenty-nine of the thirty-three men were pronounced "guilty" and sentenced to death by hanging.

Meanwhile, on the morning of November 5, Governor Johnson personally led the four disguised vessels to engage the pirates who lay in wait for the "merchant" ships. When the pirates attacked, Johnson returned fire. Quickly realizing the trap, the attackers turned for the open sea but were unable to make their getaway. Johnson's ships closed in and resumed battle. Hours later, Johnson's volunteer band boarded one of the pirate ships, killed many of the crew including the captain, and took the rest as prisoners. They chased the second ship into open sea and by mid-afternoon had routed these renegades as well. All told, twenty-six pirates had been slain, and nineteen were taken back to Charles Towne to await trial. When the governor and his crew returned to the wharves with their quarry in tow, an elated and grateful crowd was there to meet them.

Colonel Rhett and his posse also were successful in recapturing Stede Bonnet on nearby Sullivan's Island shortly after his escape; poor weather conditions had kept Bonnet and his accomplices from making a longer getaway. On November 8 Bonnet's condemned crew were hanged, and their bodies were left to dangle in the South Carolina sun for days for all to see (eventually the rotting corpses were buried in the shallow marsh off White Point at the tip of the peninsular city).

This display sent a dramatic and unmistakable message to any passing pirates that Charles Towne would no longer tolerate their treachery.

Captain Bonnet was brought to trial in Justice Trott's court two days later. Just as his men had been without counsel, Bonnet pleaded his own case, claiming that he had never intended to be a pirate but that his crew had forced *him* into piracy. His weak self-defense amidst the town's atmosphere of retribution expedited the verdict of "guilty" and a sentence of death by hanging. Governor Johnson set the execution date for December 10, 1718.

"The Gentleman Pirate" was stunned at this turn of fate and sent urgent appeals to the governor promising to "voluntarily put it out of my power to return to the ways of piracy by separating all my limbs from body, only reserving the use of my tongue to call continually on, and pray to the Lord my God, and mourn all my days in sackcloth and ashes." Several townspeople came forward to beg for his pardon, citing the reasons that Bonnet was "a man of honor, a man of fortune, and one that had a liberal education." Even Colonel Rhett offered to escort Bonnet to England for a change of venue for a new trial. The governor was unmoved.

On the morning of December 10, a terrified, trembling Stede Bonnet was taken to White Point in shackles, clutching a bouquet of wilted flowers. With the noose placed over his head, he was pushed off a horse-drawn cart and died a torturous death of strangulation. His body was left to hang for days before he too was buried in the marsh off White Point, sending a strong warning to all his cohorts flying the black banner of the skull and crossbones. Thus, the execution of Stede Bonnet marked the end of the colony's plague of piracy. His career on the high seas had accounted for the capture of thirteen ships and the killing of eighteen men.

These days, White Point Gardens by The Battery is a favorite destination with locals and visitors alike. On any day one can find children climbing on Civil War–era cannons, dogs chasing Frisbees, and couples strolling hand in hand or relaxing on benches enjoying the gentle breezes and Charleston Harbor vista. But this pleasant and serene setting under moss-draped oaks belies some of its grisly eighteenth-century history. As a White Point Gardens marker notes, NEAR THIS SPOT IN THE AUTUMN OF 1718, STEDE BONNET, NOTORIOUS "GENTLEMAN PIRATE" AND TWENTY-NINE OF HIS MEN . . . MET THEIR JUST DESERTS, leaving their legacy of adventure and terror to South Carolina's colorful history.

Dr. Lining's Weather Observations

· 1738 ·

The bells in the steeple of St. Philip's rang out their noon tidings over Charlestown as Dr. Lining looked up from his book of scientific essays. He could hear the bells clearly from his home nearby. He closed his book, carefully marking his place with a handy piece of twine, and walked to the door. Outside, King Street was a beehive of activity. A carriage rumbled past his open door, and the dust kicked up by the horses settled on Dr. Lining's buckled shoes. He looked to his left toward the docks for the telltale masts of any ships newly arrived in Charlestown. John Lining was awaiting a letter from Philadelphia—from his frequent correspondent and friend, Benjamin Franklin. With the noon sun high in the sky, he knew there would be plenty of activity along the docks, and with every inbound ship came the possibility of mail.

Lining was anxious to investigate Benjamin Franklin's electrical experiments. He previously had sent several inquiries about Franklin's kite experiment and had received a detailed reply from his friend. The letter answered Lining's queries about the equipment and the process involved and reported on other electrical experiments that Franklin had conducted. There was more than the usual interest in lightning in Charlestown since the steeple of St. Philip's Church had been struck twice in just over a month, killing a man who was working on the bells.

Lining wrote in a letter published in 1753 in *Gentleman's Magazine*, "I have several times this season when there was an appearance of a Thunderstorm, succeeded in making Mr. Franklin's experiment with a kite, for drawing the lightning from the clouds and last Monday repeated the same with remarkable success, before many spectators."

John Lining, M.D., was born in April 1708, in the small parish of Walston, Scotland, and he immigrated to Carolina in 1730, when he was twenty-two years old. It is not definitively known where he studied medicine in Europe, but his success over his thirty-year career attested to the depth of his early training. Lining settled into his physician's practice in Charlestown, where he found doctors in high demand because of the yellow-fever and smallpox epidemics that were prevalent during this period.

Even though Charlestown was one of the most important and sophisticated cities in the British Colonies, the semitropical climate and lack of sanitation created a ripe breeding ground for fevers and disease. When Dr. Lining arrived, the city had barely recovered from one of the worst yellow-fever epidemics (in 1728), and another equally severe outbreak returned in 1732. It was reported in September of that year that eight to twelve whites, as well as a great many slaves, were buried daily due to this sweeping, deadly disease. Commerce was crippled as fearful residents retreated into their homes for fear of the spreading infections. Even the tolling of church bells was prohibited because of the frequency of funerals throughout the day. All told, Charlestown lost about 7 percent of her population to the devastating fever.

In 1738 epidemics raged again, with smallpox and whooping cough striking down 10 percent of the populace. In the summer of the following year, yellow fever returned to ravage the colony. Dr. Lining saw the yellow-fever victims endure the liver and kidney damage that was revealed through traces of blood in their vomit and urine, while their skin and eyes took on a yellowish cast. Helpless to alleviate their suffering, he saw most perish within days of contracting the disease. The severity of these epidemics and the staggering loss of life triggered the young physician to seek some answers to the cause and rapid spread of these diseases, especially yellow fever. He devoted the rest of his life to the pursuit of this research.

In June of 1739 John Lining married Sarah Hill of Hillsborough Plantation, located near Charlestown. The Hill family also owned a town house on the corner of Broad and King Streets, where it is believed that John moved prior to his marriage. It is thought that this house was the location where Dr. John Lining recorded the first weather observations in America that were made with instruments designed for that purpose. Most sources say Lining's meteorological tables of rainfall and temperature, recorded three times a day, began in January 1738.

"The ingenious Dr. Lining," as contemporary writers referred to him, possessed a complete set of the available meteorological instruments of his day. Temperatures were measured by Fahrenheit's thermometer as well as a more unusual thermometer invented by Thomas Heath of London. This instrument was divided into ninety equal parts, with 49 noted as "temperate" and 65 as the "freezing" point. Out of necessity men of science at this time often had to improvise their instruments, and Lining was no exception. He made his own instrument, of unknown description, for measuring rainfall and used a whipcord hygroscope for measuring the air's relative humidity. His instruments were contained in a large, well-ventilated box that he placed outside his bedroom window at the back of the house. It is said that Mrs. Lining appealed to him not to place it on the front of the house for appearance's sake.

In 1741 Lining mentioned his methodical weather observations in his correspondence with Lowcountry indigo planter and friend, Charles Pinckney, who was in London at the time. These letters were forwarded to the Secretary of the Royal Society of London and were published in their *Philosophical Transactions of the Royal Society* in 1742–43. This recognition of his work established John Lining as a well-respected man of science throughout Europe as well as at home in Charlestown.

Lining's observations were meticulously detailed. He recorded the clearness or amount of cloudiness in the sky, and he relied on his own senses to judge the force of the wind each day, noting that this played an important role in cooling the body by causing the evaporation of perspiration. He felt his weather observations assisted in his studies of disease.

For twelve long months Lining conducted further experiments to "discover the Influence of our different Seasons upon the Human Body." He hoped that he "might arrive at some more certain knowledge of the cause of our Epidemic Diseases, which as regularly return at their Stated Seasons, as a good Clock strikes 12 when the Sun is in the Meridian; and therefore must proceed from some general Cause operating uniformly in the returning different Seasons." Lining made meticulous measurements upon himself. He recorded his weight and pulse every day at rising (6:30 to 7:30 A.M.) and before retiring in the evening (10:00 to 10:30 P.M.). He measured all the food and drink that he consumed each day. Just as carefully he measured his urine, excrement, and perspiration, the latter by weighing his dry clothes before putting them on and again after taking them off. These measurements had to be made several times a day during the intense heat of the summer months. This arduous self-study formed the basis of the earliest experiments on human metabolism made in this country.

Meanwhile, John Lining continued his meteorological observations and sent a fifteen-year table of the quantity of rainfall in Charlestown to the Royal Society in London. He wrote that "if continued for half a century [this information], might be of use in discovering to us, the changes made in a climate by clearing the Land of its woods." One might say that this line of thinking foreshadowed our environmental concerns regarding the clear-cutting of timber in present times. The table ended in February 1753, the last known date of his weather observations. Fortunately, his colleagues continued this pursuit for several years until The Medical Society of South Carolina picked up the work from 1791 through 1862. Also the state Board of Health had begun observations as early as 1824, maintaining records until 1872. By then the Signal Corps of the U.S. Army carried on the systematic weather observations that later evolved into the work of the present day U.S. Weather Bureau. Even though Lining's instruments were not as accurate as modern ones, his observations were so assiduously noted and recorded that they compare quite favorably to contemporary standards. To a large extent he is responsible for the city of Charleston, South Carolina, possessing the longest continuous records of temperature and rainfall in the United States.

In Lining's day it was acknowledged that yellow fever subsided when cooler autumn weather arrived, but the connection between the mosquito and the disease was not made until nearly 200 years later. It was generally thought that yellow fever was an imported disease, and in 1747 an act was passed establishing quarantine restrictions for the port of Charlestown. No vessel coming from an infected area could enter the harbor until one of the port physicians, among them Dr. Lining, verified that all persons aboard were in good health. The next year Lining experienced the fourth outbreak of yellow fever since his arrival in Charlestown. He compiled a history of the disease as it appeared in 1748, *A Description of the American Yellow Fever*. He hoped that "the description of this dreadful malady, which so frequently rages like the plague in the southern part of America, is so full, that a physician may, from thence, not only form a true judgment of its nature, but likewise be able to deduce and communicate some more certain method of cure, than has hitherto been used." It was yet another example of his conscientious dedication to science at a time when much of colonial life was centered on superstition and fear. Dr. John Lining's curiosity and scientific observations contributed to the growing body of medical knowledge saving South Carolina lives and generations of Americans to come.

Indigo: Eliza's Gift of Navy Blue

· 1741 ·

Sixteen-year-old Eliza Lucas and her younger sister, Polly, had accompanied their parents to her father's newly inherited estates along Wappoo Creek near the Ashley River outside Charlestown. Like many other families arriving in the colony, they had been living on the British island of Antigua in the West Indies, where a plantation economy flourished. Eliza had been given the advantage of a modest education. She had three years of formal study at an English boarding school, which (by early colonial standards) was considered plenty—for a girl. Her two older brothers were still studying in England. Boys, of course, required a "proper" education. Eliza and her sister, however, were accustomed to plantation life, and they relished the adventure of moving to a new land.

Two of the new Lucas plantations bore names referring to the inland waterways that gave ready access to the properties long before roads were built through the wilderness. The names came from Native Americans who had fished and hunted on these lands only a generation earlier. These two plantations were known as Wappoo and Waccamaw. The other Lucas plantation was aptly called Garden Hill.

The Carolina climate was more favorable to Eliza's mother, who was frail and had suffered terribly from the heat of Antigua. Eliza was quite comfortable in this climate. She was enchanted by the ancient live oaks, with their widespread branches dressed in gently flowing moss. She found the rich flora and fauna that seemed to flourish everywhere strangely fascinating—even beautiful.

Although plantation life seemed idyllic for this adventuresome teenager with delicate features and reddish-gold hair, the excitement of Charlestown was nearby, as well. Its busy wharves were bustling with trade from the islands, and ships with luxuries, supplies, and new settlers were arriving with ever-increasing reliability. A thriving society with attractive young people and promising social events was emerging. There was little reason to believe Eliza's future would be different from that of any other planter's daughter of her time. Should she be lucky enough to survive the fevers and mysterious epidemics that swept over the colony from time to time, chances were good she would eventually marry into one of the other wealthy planter families. This was the norm for a well-born girl in South Carolina during the late 1730s.

The fortunes that could be made or lost in the growing colony of Charlestown were the concern of men, not women. And Eliza was only a youngster, at that. But suddenly, one day in 1739, an ominous letter arrived by courier that changed everything for Eliza Lucas—and eventually for the economy of the colony itself.

The letter was from the office of Antigua's Royal Governor. It simply stated that by order of His Majesty the King, Eliza's father was to return to his military regiment in the West Indies—post haste. This would leave no one to stay behind and tend to the family plantations. Major Lucas had only just begun to instruct his slaves in the clearing and development of the land into a viable rice-growing operation, and an overseer had not yet been engaged to organize the work and manage the slaves. Because the growing of rice required vast fields irrigated periodically through a complicated system of dikes and floodgates, major alterations to the landscape were necessary. Most of the dike-building was finished, but much of the more difficult land-clearing was still undone.

"Eliza, my dear," her father said gravely, "I have no choice but to entrust this awesome responsibility to you. I must leave you in charge of everything—the plantations, the slaves, your infant sister, even the health of your dear mother. I'm sorry, Eliza, but it's my sworn duty to go."

He told the stunned sixteen-year-old that if she needed help or assistance before a letter could reach him on Antigua, she should ask the owners of her neighboring plantations, Mr. Charles Pinckney or Mr. Andrew Deveaux. They had more experience as rice planters and would be able to offer sage counsel.

Eliza's carefree girlhood was suddenly over. When her father left on the next morning's tide for Charlestown to board a packet sailing to Antigua, the yoke of this terrible responsibility settled on Eliza's shoulders like a giant weight. Feeling frightened and alone, she told herself, "I promised Father I'd do my best. And that's exactly what I *shall* do."

Soon, Eliza assumed her role as plantation manager with a maturity far beyond her years. She immediately recognized one critical fact: She would need the cooperation of her father's slaves. She decided to build a nursery for the slave children and a separate infirmary for those Africans who were injured or too ill to work. She made it her business to see that her father's slaves had an adequate diet, as well. These humanitarian efforts (not universally extended to colonial-era slaves) resulted in Eliza's gaining the respect and general support of her critical labor force.

Eliza's mother, who was feeling a little stronger by now, was less than pleased to see her daughter doing the hard work of a man. But Eliza was stubborn in her devotion to her beloved father; the two shared an uncommon bond. Just as she promised to do, she arose at dawn and inspected all three of the Lucas plantations before noon, meeting with newly hired overseers to discuss the day's work in the rice fields. In the afternoons she studied the reports from her overseers and wrote lengthy descriptions of their progress in letters she sent off to her father on Antigua. She kept a daily journal of her accomplishments and even found time to teach her young sister and some of the slave children music and reading. She was rarely idle.

One day, about a month after Eliza had assumed these unlikely duties, a package arrived from Major Lucas in the West Indies. With it was a letter explaining, "Darling Eliza, talk here is that indigo has done very well in Jamaica, and I am anxious that you try and grow it in South Carolina. Here is an adequate supply of the necessary seed."

Indigo was an odd, asparagus-like plant that was mostly grown in the colonies of Spain and France farther south in the Caribbean. Its leaves and stems, when processed exactly right, produced a deep-blue vegetable dye that could be sold in England, where it was used in large quantities to dye the Royal Navy's woolen uniforms, among other textiles. No one had ever successfully grown indigo in the Province of South Carolina. Eliza's neighbor, Mr. Deveaux, had tried earlier with no real success. This was a colony whose economic forte was the growing of rice, or "Carolina Gold," as it was called.

Major Lucas hoped it might be grown on the higher, drier land beyond the low-lying rice fields of the South Carolina Lowcountry. If it could be done at all, this had the potential to add a new item to the list of Lucas plantation products. It might even have larger ramifications as a profitable new export, another cash crop for South Carolina.

Although the financial benefits of introducing indigo were clear, the details of how to accomplish this were not. Even if indigo would grow in the sandy loam of the South Carolina Lowcountry, there were other factors betting against bringing in a successful crop. In the Lowcountry's semitropical climate, the threat of late-spring frost was a problem. And there seemed to be plagues of hungry insects—grasshoppers and caterpillars—ready to emerge from nowhere and attack the tender, young plants.

Also, the processing of indigo was a nasty, labor-intensive endeavor. The stems and leaves had to be soaked for long periods in large, smelly vats of hot water mixed with animal urine and lime until the dye was released into the liquid. The odor was horrendous. Then, the mix had to be boiled or precipitated until the remaining mudlike residue could be scraped off into broad, flat molds. This was dried and cut into cakes, then shipped to markets across the ocean. The task was daunting, at best.

For Eliza learning this work was largely a process of trial and error. Her entire first year's effort ended in failure. She wrote to her father, "Perhaps I harvested the plants too soon, or maybe the temperature in the vats was too warm—or too cold. But Father, let me try again. Next year, I intend to plant the seeds sooner. Let's see what difference that makes."

The following spring—a little earlier than in the previous year—Eliza planted her indigo seed, and by June it appeared the plants would produce enough leaves for a test crop. Eliza and the slaves had to check each plant daily for caterpillars. Eventually they learned to let chickens roam in the indigo fields and do this job for them. By August it was time to harvest and process the dye.

The heat was sweltering that summer as fires were constantly maintained beneath giant vats. But Eliza stayed at her task. This time the temperatures were correct. When the heavy juice was finally extracted from the indigo stems and leaves, the color was a deep "navy blue." Success hadn't come easily, nor was indigo immediately profitable. After several years of experimentation and hard work, Eliza's first indigo crop amounted to only seventeen pounds of dye. It was 1741, and Eliza Lucas was just nineteen.

News of the successful growing of indigo in South Carolina quickly spread throughout the colony, and even in

Britain, news of Eliza's success was hailed with some excitement. Parliament had been spending 150,000 pounds sterling each year to buy indigo from the colonies of Spain and France. They were willing to pay a handsome bounty for indigo grown in "their own" colony. In 1748 they authorized a guaranteed subsidy of sixpence per pound for the dried blocks of dark-blue dye.

When the French and Indian War (1756–1763) made it even more difficult for British textile manufacturers to obtain indigo from West Indian sources, the result was a bonanza for South Carolina planters. At the height of this wartime boom, South Carolina produced and shipped a million pounds of dye to Mother England. Lowcountry planters were getting rich off indigo—while it lasted.

Shortly after Eliza's success with indigo, Col. Charles Pinckney, her closest neighbor, became a widower. In time he and Eliza grew close, and although he was nineteen years her senior, they eventually married and had two sons and a daughter. Eliza never stopped experimenting with new and alternative sources of income for her plantations. She worked with silkworms and planted various tropical fruit trees and flowers, many sent to her by her mother and sister, who had rejoined her father on Antigua.

Eliza and Colonel Pinckney moved to England for several years while their sons received their formal education. But soon after their return home, Colonel Pinckney succumbed to an outbreak of malaria.

But alas, the political upheaval of the American Revolution brought a sudden end to the era of indigo in South Carolina. The war abruptly canceled the critical price subsidy, and the crop was no longer grown in any volume. Nevertheless, for a time indigo was an extremely important cash crop for the colony, second only to rice in the wealth and prosperity it provided.

Eliza Lucas was only a girl of sixteen when destiny called.

Hers was supposed to be a life of privilege and ease in the fast-growing English colony in the Carolinas. But circumstances beyond her control plus her strong will to succeed gave this daughter of a colonial landholder an important role to play in the early economy of South Carolina. Eliza died in 1793 in Philadelphia and was buried in St Peter's churchyard. One of the pallbearers at her funeral (by his own request) was a man who greatly admired Eliza's legendary charm and impressive list of accomplishments. His name was George Washington.

Francis Marion, "the Swamp Fox"
• 1780 •

The swampy lowland that lies between the Pee Dee and Santee Rivers in eastern South Carolina is thick with forest, scrubby tangled undergrowth, and hidden pools of quicksand. This dimly lit and mysterious lair is avoided, even now, by travelers unprepared to deal with its many dangers. During the American Revolution this same country served as the backdrop for the legendary adventures of Gen. Francis Marion, better known as "the Swamp Fox." The truth about the man celebrated in story, song, epic poem, and even on the motion-picture screen is somewhat different from the myth. In fact, his entrance onto the stage of military fame was fairly undignified.

Francis Marion was serving as lieutenant colonel in the Continental Army when the British forces captured Charlestown on May 12, 1780. Instead of distinguishing himself as a hero in the battle, he missed the action completely, as he happened to be attending a party in a Charlestown tavern at the time, which was hosted by his good friend, Capt. Alexander McQueen. Because heavy drinking of "spirits" was involved, Captain McQueen had instructed the tavern keeper to bolt all the doors so that his guests could freely imbibe and enjoy the fine wine he'd provided. When news arrived that the British were closing in, the guests not only were in no shape to fight, but they were also locked in! Finding no door unlocked through which he could escape, he unceremoniously jumped from a second-story window and subsequently broke his ankle in the fall. He only managed to elude the British soldiers by limping away into the night with the help of his trusted slave, Oscar.

Marion and his slave found themselves hiding out in the nearby swamps while he recuperated from this narrow escape. But this experience may have been a blessing in disguise. Had he been on duty at the time, he almost certainly would have been forced to surrender with his men and, as a Tory officer, suffer imprisonment or execution. Also, Marion's time of hiding in the swamps gave him the opportunity to learn survival skills and "new" tactics of warfare that would later on create the legend of "the Swamp Fox."

At a time when war, however brutal and bloody in reality, was still fought under formal rules of engagement that were almost gentlemanly, Francis Marion chose to take a different tack. He used stealth and cunning; he mastered the strike-and-run ambush, knowing it was better to live and fight another day. He is credited with almost single-handedly "inventing" modern guerilla warfare. Thus, Francis Marion was a man forced upon the stage of history by chance, a role he never sought for himself or his legacy.

By all accounts he was physically unimpressive: shorter than average, knock-kneed, and hook-nosed. He had piercing black eyes that looked out from a swarthy complexion. As a soldier, he was anything but a conventional role model. Many of his contemporary officers described him as sour, unpleasant, and at times a brutal disciplinarian to his men. He had reason to be, for most of his military career he was badly paid, underequipped, and largely overlooked for his innate military savvy.

Marion was born about 1731, a descendant of Huguenot refugees. He grew up in the Santee area with other members of South Carolina's early landed gentry, and he became a slave-owning rice planter. Like other such men, it was expected that he become involved in politics and serve as an officer in the local militia. He fought in the Indian wars and, for a time, he was actually a lieutenant under the famous William Moultrie. No record of his performance in those battles survives, however.

In 1775 he was elected to the State Provincial Congress and named captain in the Second Regiment of the Continental Army. He is sometimes mentioned for his military exploits in the Battle of Fort Moultrie, but modern historians say those reports are somewhat exaggerated.

Following Marion's narrow escape from the British in 1780, he and a small band of ragtag rebels had traveled into North Carolina where they met up with Gen. Horatio Gates and his Southern Army. Here was an opportunity for Marion to reenter South Carolina with the support of a conventional military force and have another chance to properly engage the British. But Gates found Marion and his rough-looking compatriots a bit unseemly for his unit, so he sent them on ahead as scouts and then subsequently marched his Southern Army headlong into a major defeat at Camden. Once again, Marion sidestepped almost certain disaster through sheer luck.

Meanwhile, deep in the Pee Dee forests, a small group of Whigs had found shelter from the British by hiding out in the swamps. Marion received orders to organize these men into a formal brigade and harass the British, who were led by Sir Banastre Tarleton ("Bloody Tarleton"). It was Tarleton who gave Marion his moniker as a "Swamp Fox."

"Fox" was an apt description of the man and his newfound military talents. He was cautious, suspicious, and cunning. He was always on the move. Time and again, Marion and his men would strike against Tarleton's troops and retreat into the safety of the Pee Dee forests. Tarleton frequently caught up with Marion's trail, but he dared not lead his men into the dark and featureless swamp where, as he put it, "the devil himself . . . could not catch this damned old fox."

Even if the life of Francis Marion seems to borrow a page

from the story of Robin Hood, and Marion's swampy hideaway seems reminiscent of Sherwood Forest, the reality was far less romantic. The men of Marion's brigade were mostly unruly volunteers who had been in the habit of coming and going at will. Sometimes they numbered as many as 200; at other times there were only thirty. Discipline and order were not their forte.

Marion's ability to inspire and lead such a motley crew was no small feat. Although some men said he was "fair" and even "merciful" in his dealings with behavioral problems, a few of Marion's military record books survive and recount how up to one quarter of the men in the Second South Carolina Regiment received court-martial-ordered lashings with a "cat o'nine tails." As many as 500 lashes were administered on some men for such infractions as neglect of duty, drunkenness, and being absent without leave.

Marion developed the art of being an intelligence officer. He had a sophisticated network of scouts and informers strung throughout his area of operation. He preferred to travel after dusk and ride all night, sometimes covering up to 70 miles at a time. This nomadic, horseback existence was punctuated by brief but violent skirmishes with the British. The men slept in the open swamp, with little more than a blanket for shelter. Provisions were scarce, and ammunition was always in short supply. Their diet consisted mostly of sweet potatoes and whatever wild game they could kill. Occasionally, they would happen across some range cattle and steal a taste of beef. More often, a quick and cold meal was the norm. (Cooking fires might betray their location.) Then it was on to the next hidden camp.

Even basic clothing was a problem. Most of Marion's men wore homespun garments, and most of his officers had only a single shirt. Once, a campfire got out of hand, and Marion's kit caught fire. His leather helmet (part of his original Second Regiment uniform) was partially burned, as was his only blanket. For the best part of the next year, he made do with half a blanket against the cold and what amounted to only half a hat. As ragged as "the Swamp Fox" and his men must have looked, each one wore a dashing white feather in his cap, a mark of distinction that immediately identified them to friend and foe alike.

Actually, Marion's military role in the Revolution was limited to a number of troublesome raids and minor skirmishes, but he became important to the cause of independence for another reason. Not the least of his contributions was the inspiration he gave other Revolutionary patriots. His unconventional military tactics remained a thorn in the side of the British at a time when, militarily, the British were in control of South Carolina. Francis Marion's daring band of Whig rebels quickly became legendary, even in his own time. Ironically, not a single account exists of Marion ever personally raising his sword in combat. His brilliance seems to have been in his leadership.

Following the British defeat at the Battle of Yorktown in October 1781 and Cornwallis's surrender, the war raged on in South Carolina for another two bloody years. Through it all Marion stayed in the field. The newly organized state government sang his praises, but it failed to reward him financially. Somehow he maintained the will to fight, but not without periods of discouragement and even despair. There were times when the strain made him brood and even threaten to resign his commission.

The Revolutionary War in South Carolina was a long and ugly ordeal. It was rife with petty personal vendettas among officers, indiscriminant house burnings, looting, and murder as everyday events. Francis Marion had seen more than his share of it. Peace negotiations were under way when he fought his last battle at Wadboo Creek on November 16, 1782. He felt enough blood had been shed in the name of freedom, and he was finished with war.

He returned to his plantation on the Santee River, Pond Bluff, to find it in ruins. There, with a few slaves, he slowly began to rebuild the world he knew before the war. He married late in life and lived out his days quietly, most notably serving as a state senator and performing leadership roles in small official capacities.

Francis Marion died at the age of sixty-three on February 27, 1795, and is buried beside his wife at Belle Isle Plantation in present-day Berkeley County, about 10 miles west of St. Stephen. His grave bears this tribute: HISTORY WILL RECORD HIS WORTH AND RISING GENERATIONS WILL EMBALM HIS MEMORY AS ONE OF THE MOST DISTINGUISHED PATRIOTS AND HEROES OF THE AMERICAN REVOLUTION.

Rebecca Motte and the Flaming Arrows

· 1781 ·

She was a lady—first and foremost—born to wealth, power and prestige. Yet here she was, caught up in the violent conflicts of a man's world: a bloody revolution for political and economic independence and the cruel tactics of eighteenth-century warfare. "How did I ever get here!" she must have thought as she found herself actually standing between opposing forces of the American Revolution at the Battle of Fort Motte, on the brink of immortality as a heroine of the war, her sex, and her beloved country.

Rebecca Brewton Motte was a wealthy widow of forty-three when, in 1781, she was living with her daughters at her grandfather's plantation on the south side of the Congaree River known as "Buckhead." At this remote location near present-day Lake Marion, she hoped to avoid the physical dangers of the American War of Independence. But she watched helplessly as the British army approached on horseback and a stern-looking Lieutenant McPherson dismounted and announced his plans to occupy the house. He wanted to use it as a fort to augment British supply lines from Charlestown—already under their control. There was little the lone woman could do to stop him.

Almost immediately, men were dispatched by McPherson to throw up fortifications around the house and grounds, dig

ditches through the formal gardens and chop down rare, orna-
mental trees to open vistas for surveillance. The place would
be renamed "Fort Motte," and as a special favor to the mistress
in residence, she would be allowed to stay on in a small nearby outbuilding and serve as cook and "hostess" to the officers
of occupation in the main house.

This was not Rebecca's first encounter with the British
army or with the staff of elite officers who played key roles in
the fall of Charlestown. As the sister of wealthy Charlestown
merchant Miles Brewton, she had inherited her brother's opu-
lent King Street mansion following his untimely death at sea in
1715. Because the fabulous Miles Brewton House was (and still
is) considered one of the finest homes in America, it followed
that this fine Georgian house would serve as headquarters for
Sir Henry Clinton throughout the British occupation.

Rebecca's late husband, Jacob Motte, had served as
provincial treasurer for many years, so she was allowed to
remain in her Charlestown residence. Because her sympathies
and loyalties had been decidedly on the side of the patriots
since the earliest days of the war, however, Rebecca was essentially made a captive in her own home. A true lady, she made
the best of an unpleasant situation, behaving like a gracious
hostess to her uninvited guests. For weeks on end she presided
over her sumptuous dining-room table while Clinton, Lord
Francis Rawdon, and even General Cornwallis himself dined
lavishly from the well-stocked Brewton larder.

Tradition says that while Rebecca entertained the British
officers downstairs, she secretly hid her three young daughters
in the attic to spare them any dangerous interaction with the
men. Although the British soldiers were not supposed to know
anything about the Motte girls' presence, apparently the frequent comings and goings of house servants gave Clinton reason to suspect Rebecca's ruse. But because Rebecca's behavior
was so genial and charming, the interlopers allowed this cha-
rade to go on for months.

Finally, Rebecca found an excuse to "remove herself" from Charlestown, supposedly to look after the family holdings of her late grandfather at Buckhead Plantation. There, she hoped to escape further personal contact with the occupation forces while the uncertain fate of the Revolution played itself out through the fortunes of war. As Rebecca stepped into the carriage that would take her and her household retinue away from the city into the relative safety of the country, Clinton is reported to have whispered something to Rebecca as he smiled and bid her good-bye. "How unfortunate it is," he is supposed to have said as he looked up at the ceiling, "that I've been unable to meet the . . . 'rest of the family.'"

Rebecca had hoped for peace and safety at Buckhead, but now it was all happening again. With the arrival of McPherson and his men, she was once more physically displaced and forced to serve the British officers as they systematically made a wreck of her home.

British reinforcements arrived to help transform Buckhead into Fort Motte. By May of 1781 Fort Motte housed a total of 150 Tory soldiers, a significant force at the time. Even as the number of enemy soldiers grew, Rebecca maintained her poise. She realized she was surrounded and completely at their mercy. She organized her servants to cook and serve the British officers with every courtesy possible. Again, she presided over her table with the dignity and calm of a great lady, even enduring insults and sometimes rowdy behavior. At night she was allowed to retreat to the small outbuilding that served as her private quarters, until the next day's meal was supposed to appear on her dining table to appease the British officers' appetites.

Rebecca's courage and restraint paid off in that her life was never overtly threatened. And there was another plus; it bought her precious time. Although she didn't know it, help was on the way.

American forces under the leadership of Gen. Francis

Marion, the notorious "Swamp Fox," and "Lighthorse" Harry Lee were approaching Fort Motte with orders to capture the British garrison and eliminate this supply hub to the enemy's war effort. As they stealthily advanced toward the fortification, which was bustling with daytime activity and fresh reinforcements, it was clear the Americans were outnumbered. Marion had only one artillery piece with him, and to lay effective siege against the fort, he would have to employ some clever element of surprise.

Marion's men quietly dug trenches along a natural ravine near the house, and servants passed word to Rebecca that "the Swamp Fox" lay in wait. It was crucial they remain unseen until the last moment before the attack, but before they could make their move, word came that even more British troops were on their way; Lord Rawdon was bringing his men in from Camden for re-supply. Marion had to act fast.

Marion decided that if they could set fire to the house, the ensuing confusion and the distraction of fighting the fire would provide them the cover for a surprise attack. As a gentleman, Francis Marion felt obligated to seek Mrs. Motte's permission before setting her house on fire. He quickly told her of his plan, and she reportedly replied, "Do not hesitate for a moment, sir! I shall give you something to facilitate the destruction, myself."

With that she brought out three "fire arrows" that had been gifts to her grandfather from Rebecca's late husband. An East Indian sea captain supposedly had made these strange arrows in such a way that they would ignite upon striking their target. It is said she even provided the bow with which to shoot them.

The hot, dry, wooden shingles of the roof made a perfect target, and soon the fire was ablaze. Just as Marion had intended, the British furiously began tearing off the shingles to save the house. Marion's men had, by now, aimed their artillery so as to frustrate these efforts.

Lieutenant McPherson recognized his dilemma. If he

fought the fire, Marion's artillery would pick off his men. If he let the fire burn, Fort Motte would be lost and his men would be defenseless. He had no choice but to surrender.

Once the flag of surrender was shown, both the British and Marion's men worked feverishly to put out the fire. Amazingly, supposed "enemies" actually cooperated and managed to quell the flames, and a substantial portion of Rebecca's plantation house was saved. That night, as the roof embers still smoldered, Rebecca Motte served a hearty meal to the officers on both sides of the conflict, in gratitude for their sensibility and generosity in saving her home.

Meanwhile, an incredulous Lord Rawdon witnessed the entire affair. He had just arrived across the river but could not ford the waters in time to intervene. Rawdon moved on south toward Moncks Corner while Marion slipped away to continue his attacks against British outposts throughout the South Carolina midlands.

The Battle of Fort Motte was technically a victory for Marion, but in another way it was an impasse. Rebecca Motte's story became legend even before the Revolution was over. She lived on with the well-earned respect of soldiers on both sides of the conflict until her death in 1815 at the age of seventy-seven years. The role women play in warfare has continued to confuse and disarm the combatants in wars ever since.

Birthplace of American Golf

· 1786 ·

The group of children playing "hide-and-seek" among the live oaks, palmettos, and tall marsh grasses near the Ashley River at Harleston's Green was interrupted yet again by one of those pesky "finders" waving them away and calling out "Fore!" Reluctantly the children gave up their keen hiding places and slowly walked rather sulkily to another part of the village green to resume their play. If they could remember by the time they returned home, they were going to tell their parents that those men in the scarlet coats were becoming bothersome.

On any nice day Harleston's Green was the scene of a wide variety of recreational activity. The space, named for property owner Capt. John Harleston, was one of Charleston's larger public greens on the peninsula bounded by Boundary (now Calhoun), Coming, and Beaufain Streets and the Ashley River. In addition to a regular number of youngsters cavorting and nurses strolling with babies, a cattle exhibition, a cricket match, or an impromptu horse race might crop up at any time. It was a popular spot and a microcosm of the leisure pursuits on the rise in post-Revolutionary Charleston.

The upper classes living in the South Carolina Lowcountry represented a very affluent segment of the newly formed country, and the plantation society was a cosmopolitan and pleasure-seeking group. All kinds of entertainment were embraced such as concerts, theater, dance assemblies, oratory, and even horse racing. It was only natural that golf, a popular leisure sport in England and Scotland, would find its way to this former colony, largely populated by English and Scottish settlers. Many of these planters and merchants frequently traveled to the old country to conduct business, and some even maintained second homes there. Wealthy South Carolinians also sent their sons to England in large numbers for a proper education so that ties remained close even after the governmental separation.

Tracing the beginnings of the game of golf as a sport is sketchy, with the debate centering on whether golf got its start in The Netherlands or Scotland. The Dutch claim is based on the fact that the word golf is thought to be derived from their word *kolf,* meaning a club; and several illustrations dating from around the beginning of the sixteenth century depict people swinging (mostly on ice) something similar to golf clubs. One in particular shows a young boy attempting to send a ball to a hole in the turf.

The Scottish claim for the origins of the game seems to predate the Dutch claim, with documentation as early as 1457. In that year the Scottish Parliament under King James II passed a law forbidding the playing of golf. It was decreed that "futeball and golfe be utterly cryded downe." Apparently, it had become so popular that Scots were devoting so much time to the game that they were actually neglecting their archery practice, which was crucial to the national defense of the country! Fourteen years later another law attempted to discourage the playing of the sport. None of this legislation met with much success however, and the Scots continued intensely pursuing the pastime and developing it into the game most closely resembling what is played today.

Whatever its beginnings as a sport, most golf authorities acknowledge that the claim of the first organized golf club and course in America belongs to Charleston, South Carolina. A shipment of 96 golf clubs and 432 golf balls from the Port of Leith, Scotland, was delivered to Charleston merchant David Deas in 1743, providing evidence of Charleston's being an active golfing community in the mid- to late-eighteenth century. The South Carolina Golf Club was formed on September 29, 1786, by a group of prosperous local merchants, primarily as a social organization. It is not even known if they played golf at the outset.

An extract from the 1793 *South Carolina and Georgia Almanac* documents a golf club formed in 1786. Notices were advertised in the *Charleston Gazette* announcing an anniversary gathering in 1791 in Williams Coffee House and again in 1794 on Harleston's Green. Additional newspaper notices dating from September 1788 stated, "There is lately erected that pleasing and genteel amusement Kolf Baan."

Experts of the game such as golf historian Charles Price dispute that Kolf Baan is "true golf" since it was played on a "walled court, usually paved and often connected to an inn. The 'kolf-baan' was used to drum up business much as golf courses today are used to lure guests to resort hotels." He also points out that the "club, of 'kolf' . . . had a straight face, which was usually composed of brass, and [was] a good deal larger and cruder than present-day golf clubs. . . . The chief difference between the equipment for 'kolven' and golf equipment was the ball, which was the size of a grapefruit and weighed almost two pounds."

As was the custom in Scotland and England, members of the South Carolina Golf Club in the late 1700s played on the common public area, or village green. The public space for this purpose in Charleston was Harleston's Green. Thus, the terms "green fees" and "greenkeeper" (not green*s* fees or green*s*keeper) are handed down from the practice of fees paid to town officials for the use of the public land. The necessity of a "finder," or forecaddy, to precede the approaching golfers and warn those walking, playing, or riding through the village green becomes apparent. "Be forewarned!" or its shortened version "Fore!" was an alert to all visitors to the green, not just fellow golfers on another hole.

The equipment of this time that most closely resembled present-day equipment were wooden-shafted clubs, similar in shape to hockey sticks, and a ball made of stitched leather stuffed with boiled chicken feathers. The ball aptly enough was called a "feathery." Irons were not widely used because of their tendency to split apart the feathery. Instead, a series of wooden clubs called "spoons"—long, mid, short, and baffling spoons—with slightly concave club heads were used to advance the ball to the hole.

In general the objective of the game was the same. The golfers (usually wearing scarlet coats for easy identification) played cross-country to reach a hole in the ground, sometimes as large as a foot across. It was an individual skill with no interference from an opponent. The opponents did determine the winner of the "round," however, because all the competitions were match play. The golfer who was a stroke or more up on his opponents at the last hole was deemed the winner. As yet the number of total strokes by a player were not tallied, and no exact number of holes were consistently designated for the match. Adding to the challenges of the game, there were no tee areas, nor were there flagsticks or putting surfaces on the course. The match started at whatever spot was chosen as the starting point aiming for the first hole. The "finder" proved useful again, as he often ran ahead and pointed out the location of the hole. After completion of each hole, another spot was selected for teeing off at a distance of two club-lengths from that hole.

In spite of these difficulties, the sport persisted, and Harleston's Green remained the local venue for a number of years. It is thought that its popularity began to decline after the enactment of the Jefferson Embargo of 1808, which restricted foreign commercial trade. Many of the Scottish merchants left

Charleston to return home. At the same time Harleston's Green was undergoing change, and residential development along Bull and Montagu Streets began infringing on the open space. Also during the 1800s leisure pursuits in the Lowcountry were interrupted repeatedly by wars, fires, and storms, as well as a severe earthquake. Still, golf refused to die out, and the next documentation appears again in 1899, when the Chicora Park Golf Club was formed. A nine-hole course with a clubhouse was situated along the west bank of the Cooper River about 6 miles north of downtown Charleston on the site of a former plantation. Just one year later, however, the United States government took over the grounds to build a new navy yard. The golf facilities were relocated a few miles away at Belvedere Plantation, just north of Magnolia Cemetery, where a nine-hole course with sand greens was opened in 1901 for a membership of 300 in what was now called The Charleston Country Club. By 1913 the sand greens were replaced with turf grass, and the course was expanded to include eighteen holes.

As this area on the northern stretch of the peninsula grew more industrialized, another location was sought for more attractive surroundings. The new location was just a bit farther removed across the Ashley River, overlooking Charleston Harbor and the city. The course was designed by noted golf architect Seth Raynor, and it opened in the spring of 1925. As a result of the Great Depression, the club went into liquidation in 1935 and was reorganized as the present-day Country Club of Charleston. The South Carolina Golf Club reemerged when it was rechartered and located at Sea Pines Plantation on Hilton Head Island, South Carolina, the site of the Heritage Golf Classic PGA event. From its humble beginnings in 1786 as the South Carolina Golf Club and Harleston's Green, "America's Birthplace of Golf" has grown into a $1.5-billion industry for the state of South Carolina, with an abundance of courses around the state enjoyed by visitors, locals, and professionals year-round. And, my, wouldn't those scarlet-coated gents be surprised!

Jonathan Lucas and "Carolina Gold"

· 1787 ·

Although the name Eli Whitney and the cotton gin are inextricably linked in the minds of most Americans, the name Jonathan Lucas and the rice mill are less familiar. But the nearly anonymous Lucas was no less significant in revolutionizing a major agricultural industry lasting from the last decade of the eighteenth through the early twentieth century in the American South.

Before the American Revolution, competing dyes, lack of an English bounty, and the disruption of trade with England during the war years had led to a decline in the once-profitable commodity of indigo, the primary colonial cash crop. Rice was now in great demand in Europe and around the world. And the coastal areas of the Carolinas and Georgia, ideally suited to the crop, responded to the markets' call.

As early as 1685 rice seed brought from Madagascar was grown in the Carolinas at primarily inland sites along the banks of freshwater rivers and swampy areas. When periods of drought devastated the crop, the need for a constant source of water became apparent. By the mid-1700s the move to tidal freshwater swamplands was made. In coastal South Carolina alone, 150,000 acres of freshwater swamp were transformed into rice fields over the next decades. Some 40,000 acres of these were located on the lowlands surrounding the rivers that converge at the port of Georgetown, South Carolina. The loamy, rich soil along the marshy areas of the Waccamaw, Pee Dee, Black, and Sampit Rivers were prime planting sites. Just a few miles to the south, the Santee River delta was another perfect setting for rice cultivation. In addition to the natural characteristics of the terrain, two other major factors contributed to the region's dominance in the rice industry.

The extensive use of slave labor was critical in clearing the swamplands and constructing and tending the rice fields. The colony was no stranger to slave labor since many of the white settlers to arrive in Charles Towne in the late seventeenth century had brought large numbers of Africans along to raise crops or harvest raw materials that they could sell to European markets. Georgetown, a port of entry since 1732, had already established an active foreign and domestic trade for shipping agricultural goods to other markets. As the colony prospered, more slaves were imported to handle the labor-intensive agrarian pursuits of the successful planters.

The mammoth task of clearing the cypress forests, digging the canals, building the rice banks, and constructing the dikes in the swampy acreage fell to the slaves, assisted only by primitive hand tools and oxen. Many people have compared the undertaking to the building of the Egyptian pyramids. Africans brought from Senegal were especially prized for this work since they brought from their homeland experience in the early technology of rice cultivation. They also seemed to have a partial immunity to the ravages of malaria, so prevalent around the low-lying wetlands. (Recent studies indicate that the hereditary sickle-cell-anemia trait in some African Americans prevents the development of malaria.)

The mechanical inventiveness of an Englishman named Jonathan Lucas was to play a major part in streamlining the processing of rice for shipment to foreign markets. The harvesting, threshing, and milling of the rice was, up until this time, also a labor-intensive, slow process. The rice was harvested from the fields by hand; then the seeds were knocked out of the plant by slaves wielding flailing sticks. Winnowing barns were erected to drop the rice down from the upper level into an open area underneath, which allowed the wind to separate the chaff from the rice. More slaves swept off the discarded matter and collected the grain. The hull and brown bran layer covering the rice had to be removed next. (Even though the bran layer made the rice a more nutritious staple, the rice would turn rancid during shipment to foreign ports, so it had to be eliminated.) Man-powered wooden mortar and pestles were used during this arduous process.

Jonathan Lucas, an educated millwright from Cumberland, England, sailed for America shortly after the Revolution and accidentally landed north of his intended destination. A storm forced an entry near the mouth of the Santee River and apparently, the ordeal of the storm convinced Lucas to remain on terra firm and begin a new life for himself there. He soon witnessed the strenuous hand processes for cleaning and preparing the rice, and his mechanical mind set to work solving the problem. Lucas came from a family of English mill owners and builders, and his expertise quickly found a sponsor in John Bowman, a rice planter and owner of Peachtree Plantation, located on the Santee. Bowman hired Lucas in 1787 to construct a waterpowered mill there, the first of its kind. Lucas harnessed waterpower to turn millstones and mechanized mortar and pestles to hull and remove the bran from the rice—a much-improved method over slaves pounding the rice with mortar and pestles by hand. Word traveled fast, and Lucas built water mills for many other planters in the district, many of whom were prominent political figures of the American Revolution. He constructed another water mill at Washo Plantation on the Santee River for Mrs. Middleton, who later became the wife of Gen. Thomas Pinckney. Another was erected for Gen. Peter Horry on his Winyah Bay property and yet another for Col. William Alston at Fairfield Plantation on the Waccamaw River.

In 1791–92 Lucas built his first tide mill powered by tidal water flow that could work automatically both day and night for Andrew Johnstone at Millbrook Plantation on the Santee. Shortly thereafter, he made improvements to the concept and erected a tide mill with elevators, rolling screens, and packers, which was quite a mechanical feat at the time. The owner of this innovative mill at Mepkin Plantation on the Cooper River near Charleston was Henry Laurens, another prominent Revolutionary War figure. During the 1790s Jonathan Lucas became a very successful mill builder, and in 1795 he constructed a combination rice mill and sawmill driven by water-power on his own recently purchased property at Haddrell's Point on Shem Creek near Charleston Harbor. He sent for his seventeen-year-old son, Jonathan Jr., to come from England to help with the prospering business. By the early 1800s Lucas and Jonathan Jr. (who later patented the process) collaborated to construct more mills around Charleston that processed rice for planters willing to pay a "toll" for the service (often using a portion of their rice for payment) rather than construct a mill of their own. Lucas was also the first to employ the use of steam to power a mill built in Charleston in 1817.

Earlier, man and animal-powered mills might beat out a mere three barrels of rice a day, but the water mills, run by only three people, could produce an average of one hundred barrels a week. Each barrel weighed up to 600 pounds each. Lucas's process rapidly propelled the rice industry to the forefront of the area's economy. By the nineteenth century an average of thirty-two million bushels of rice a year were exported from the region. By 1840 Georgetown County produced nearly one half of the rice grown in the United States. "Carolina Gold," as it was known, was prized above all other rice grown around the world. A home etiquette book published in London as early as 1776 specified "procuring only Waccamaw Gold from the Carolina" when serving rice. Vast fortunes were made, and the per capita income for

Georgetown County was the highest in the country in 1855.

For more than a century, rice dominated South Carolina's coastal economy, and the grandeur it fostered was evident in the elegant plantation mansions, town houses, and gardens built throughout the region. The influential planter families enjoyed all the luxuries of the time. They were well-educated and well-traveled, embellishing their homes with the finest of European furnishings and savoring fine wines and imported delicacies. They raised thoroughbred horses and embraced the "social season" of parties in Charleston during the winter months.

Eventually, a series of events would contribute to the demise of the rice culture in South Carolina. During the Civil War international trade was disrupted, and the planters never fully recovered their lucrative overseas markets. The abolishment of slavery eradicated the cheap labor force, and many of the former slaves migrated to northern cities in search of better opportunity. A series of major storms like the hurricanes of 1893, 1903, 1906, and the back-to-back years of 1910 and 1911 devastated the rice fields. After that the lack of manpower was an even more serious problem when faced with rebuilding the fields. And further improvements in mechanization led to more competition in other states like Louisiana, Arkansas, and Texas. Georgetown County saw its last commercial rice harvest in 1919, marking the end of the "Carolina Gold" rice empire for South Carolina.

The agricultural legacy Jonathan Lucas fostered lives on, however, in the grand town homes in Georgetown, Charleston, and Beaufort and in the magnificent plantations that supported them. Still in evidence are traces of old rice fields built and maintained by back-breaking slave labor. Although the heyday of rice is long past, the vast industry it spawned in South Carolina has been supplanted by an even bigger one—an industry called tourism.

When President Washington Came to Call

· 1791 ·

A crowd was gathering along the waterfront of Georgetown, South Carolina, on the morning of April 30, 1791. After months of preparation the first president of the United States, George Washington, was due to arrive any time. Well-wishers young and old could hardly contain their excitement. Mothers had brought their children to get a glimpse of the great man. Revolutionary War veterans turned out to pay their respects to their venerated commander-in-chief. All citizens, none sure what to expect or what was expected of them, wanted to be a part of the festivities and welcome President Washington in a way befitting the leader of a new democratic nation.

Of course, they had no precedent, other than what some may have known of royal protocol, as to how this man should be received. As described by Terry Lipscomb in *South Carolina in 1791: George Washington's Southern Tour,* President Washington found himself and his retinue greeted very grandly over the next weeks on his trip through the state. In Georgetown the reception committee dispatched a flotilla to meet the official party as they arrived down the Waccamaw River. Washington himself was transported in "an elegant painted boat" rowed by seven ship captains attired in blue topcoats, white jackets, and golden-lace-trimmed hats. As the boats approached their landing at Market Square, they were greeted by a fifteen-gun federal salute, each gun representing a state in the newly formed nation. (At the time there were only fourteen states, but Kentucky was set to join the following year, so the artillerymen throughout Washington's tour fired fifteen guns in anticipation of that event.)

Washington's party was equally impressive in their finery. His entourage consisted of a new, cream-colored, elegant traveling coach that Southerners would later recall as the president's "white chariot." Four reddish-brown, black-maned bay horses were chosen to draw the new coach. As his personal mount Washington selected Prescott, a dignified and majestic white charger that he often used as his parade horse back in Philadelphia, the current capital of the United States. Prescott was usually outfitted with a silver-mounted saddle and a gold-trimmed saddlecloth, and the 6-foot-3-inch president made a striking appearance when he arrived at each new destination wearing his Continental Army uniform.

Accompanying Washington was his private secretary and traveling companion, Maj. William Jackson, who was well connected in South Carolina and who proved to be an invaluable political liaison. Other staff on the trip included a coachman, a valet, two footmen, a postilion, and slaves who drove the baggage wagon. The final member of the expedition was Cornwallis, Washington's favorite pet greyhound.

The Southern Tour was an ambitious and somewhat risky endeavor for the first president of the United States, who had been inaugurated only two years earlier. Many questioned the wisdom of the decision for the young nation's leader to leave behind his executive duties and his oversight of foreign affairs for such a long trip. The trip would encompass more than 1,800 difficult miles, and communication was slow and unreliable. The roads and bridges connecting the country—in many areas still a backwoods—were primitive and dangerous. A good day's travel might cover a distance of 25 to 30 miles. And Washington's health had been precarious since his bout with pneumonia in May 1790.

So why attempt such an arduous trip? The president had what he considered some compelling reasons. This gentleman farmer, military leader, and statesman wanted "to acquire knowledge of the face of the Country, the growth and Agriculture thereof" and to see "how far the Country is recovered from the ravages of war." He hoped "to become better acquainted with their [the states'] principal Characters and internal Circumstances and . . . be more accessible to numbers of well-informed persons, who might give him useful information and advices on political subjects."

In addition to its value for fact-finding, his mission was an early "public relations tour" that would help to unify the populace behind their new central government. Some citizens were suspicious of central authority, and the new constitution had fallen under criticism for not including a bill of rights, an omission rectified in December 1791. Washington also used the opportunity to seek out potential candidates from the southern region for positions within the new government. And lastly, he believed that a renewed active lifestyle, as he wrote to his friend, the Marquis de Lafayette, would actually improve his health.

At the ceremonial welcome in Georgetown, President Washington was greeted "by a Company of Infantry handsomely uniformed" who presented arms and followed his inspection with a firing of musket rounds. He received a "congratulatory address" from the reception committee, a ritual of etiquette in every town that he visited. They respectfully professed their admiration for "the first Magistrate of the Federal Republic" and retold the stories of their duress during the Revolution. On his processional walk through the streets of Georgetown, he observed both the postwar recovery and the scars of destruction left over from the British burning of the community.

Washington acknowledged their sufferings and fortitude, expressing the nation's gratitude. At four o'clock that afternoon, he attended a formal dinner where he was seated at the place of honor, a chair bedecked with an arch of laurel blossoms. Over the course of the evening, at least fifteen eloquent toasts were offered, exemplified by one: "May the nations of the earth enjoy an equal happiness with us in having rulers equally sedulous to make themselves acquainted with the true interests and situations of the people."

After dinner he was entertained at a tea party by more than fifty ladies of Georgetown, many of whom wore sashes bearing images of the American eagle and the Latin words "E Pluribus Unum." Here, another laurel-decorated chair was offered, but the president politely declined in favor of gallantly seating several ladies in turn while conversing with them. The day's events were capped off with a grand ball, where additional elegantly dressed ladies from town as well as the surrounding large rice plantations wore bandeaus inscribed with WELCOME THE HERO and LONG LIFE TO THE PRESIDENT. At the end of the evening, he was escorted back to the "elegant house" (now called the Stewart-Parker house, still standing on Front Street) that had been prepared for his stay. The president had been adamant about paying for his accommodations—either public or private—throughout his trip. He wanted to avoid the appearance of playing favorites among the local citizenry.

Hampton Plantation, home of Harriott Pinckney Horry, was his next stop along the South Carolina coast, on the morning of May 1. Mrs. Horry was the widow of Col. Daniel Horry, rice planter and Revolutionary War cavalryman, and the daughter of Eliza Lucas Pinckney, well-known indigo cultivator. Both women, along with Harriott's daughter and several nieces, received the president, escorted by Harriott's brother, Maj. Thomas Pinckney, onto the large, Adam-style, white-columned portico, completed just prior to Washington's visit. Again, each wore patriotic sashes displaying his portrait along with the great seal. Mrs. Horry hosted a stately reception attended by many of her friends and neighbors, who then adjourned into the elegant, blue-ceilinged, 700-square-foot ballroom for a sumptuous breakfast.

During his daylong visit Mrs. Horry consulted her famous guest on a landscaping dilemma. Her late husband had used the front lawn as a horse racing track, keeping it clear of any trees. A young live oak had sprouted in front of the house, and she was considering its removal. Washington advised her to "keep the oak," and now, more than 200 years later, the "Washington Oak" still graces the front lawn. (Both Hampton Plantation and the "Washington Oak" can be seen by the public at this South Carolina State Park.)

The stops in Georgetown and Hampton Plantation were only two of the interesting and productive visits on the president's South Carolina itinerary. He spent an entire week in Charleston, where he was celebrated, toasted, paraded, applauded, and entertained. The fifty-nine-year-old Virginia gentleman even recorded in his usually laconic diary that precisely 256 "elegantly dressed & handsome ladies" had attended a "very elegant dancing Assembly." The following evening "at least 400 ladies the number and appearance of wch. exceeded any thing of the kind I had ever seen."

In between processionals and social engagements, he toured the battlefields of Charleston, guided by leading local veterans such as Col. Charles Cotesworth Pinckney, Capt. Edward Rutledge, and Gen. William Moultrie, who had played a key role in the city's defenses and the outcome of the war.

Escorted by prominent citizens of Charleston for a number of miles out of the city, Washington and his entourage headed south toward Savannah. Along the way he stopped at Sandy Hill, the plantation home of his cousin, William Washington, where George, the gentleman farmer, no doubt studied the workings of a productive rice plantation. Another notable stop was a visit at White Hall plantation, home of Judge Thomas Heyward, a signer of the Declaration of Independence and absentee owner of the town home where Washington had lodged in Charleston. From White Hall he traveled to Purrysburg, a former Yemassee Indian settlement, where a delegation escorted him on to Georgia.

Returning later to South Carolina, he journeyed through the "pine barren" of the Midlands to "Columbia, the newly adopted Seat of the Government of South Carolina," escorted by Wade Hampton, esteemed Revolutionary War veteran, planter, and businessman, and Thomas Taylor, one of the founders of the city. After touring the House and Senate chambers, he dined at a large public dinner at the new State House designed by James Hoban, who later designed the White House.

He met dozens of South Carolinians from the surrounding towns of Orangeburg, Winnsboro, Belleville, Stateburg, Granby, and Camden. At Camden he examined the Revolutionary War battlefields, evaluating the tactics of Gen. Nathaniel Greene and Lord Francis Rawdon at Hobkirk Hill and Gen. Horatio Gates and Lord Cornwallis at the Battle of Camden "which terminated so unfavourably for the former."

Washington and his party traveled on through Kershaw, Lancaster, and York Counties, finally departing South Carolina on May 28, 1791, and heading toward Charlotte, North Carolina. As he did, he must have felt a sense of accomplishment that many of his goals for this segment of his Southern Tour had been achieved. He had attained a greater knowledge of the terrain, agriculture, and prosperity of the state. He witnessed many of the major Revolutionary War battle sites, their destructive aftermath, and emerging recovery. He established many important contacts and became better acquainted with numerous leaders of the region and, no doubt, received much advice on the political issues of the day. His trip had served to unify the country, reinforcing South Carolinians' belief that they would have a significant voice in the course of the new democracy.

Denmark Vesey: Martyr of Slavery

· 1822 ·

Denmark Vesey put the kettle on to make a cup of coffee. He sat down at the kitchen table to contemplate the stack of crisp bills lined up before him. He couldn't believe all this money was really his. The chances of his ever having a fortune like this were about the same as winning the lottery, and, that's exactly what had happened. His prize was $1,500—more money than he had ever seen in his life. Clearly, winning the municipal lottery marked the beginning of a new life for this black man.

Denmark Vesey was born in 1767 on St. Thomas in the Virgin Islands. The events and experiences of his young life laid the groundwork for the mission of this future rebel. At age fourteen he was taken aboard a slave ship bound for the French colony of St. Domingue by Capt. Joseph Vesey. In St. Domingue the young captive was sold to a sugarcane planter, with whom he stayed for several months, until April 1782. When his new owner suspected him of having epilepsy—it was required by law that a slave seller repurchase any unfit slave— Denmark became the captain's personal servant and took on the surname of Vesey. During this time he learned to read and write under Captain Vesey's tutelage.

Captain Vesey was heavily engaged in the slave trade between the Caribbean islands and the African coast, success- fully garnering large profits from the high demand for male slave labor on the sugarcane plantations of the islands. Growing sugarcane, like tobacco in Virginia and rice in South Carolina, was labor intensive and a year-round operation in the tropical climate. On St. Domingue alone, French colonists imported as many as 20,000 slaves annually during the height of the demand for sugar in the 1770s.

From 1781 to 1783 Denmark accompanied his master on voyages throughout the Caribbean and to the coast of West Africa. Here he was witness to the dealings of Joseph Vesey as a slave trader. Captain Vesey, like so many slave traders before and after him, expertly examined each man, woman, and child as one might scrutinize a horse or some other piece of property. He selected only those who appeared most fit to withstand the journey and who would bring a good price. Denmark watched as these humans were bartered in exchange for rum, sugar, salt, cloth, tobacco, gunpowder, knives, and other products. Once on board, the ship's crew forced the new slaves below deck, where they were chained side by side, body to body. They remained in this condition for most of the journey across the Atlantic. Between a quarter and a third of the "cargo" perished from disease or suicide.

By the age of sixteen, Denmark had seen firsthand the torturous punishments of branding irons, whips, and thumbscrews for any who attempted defiance or escape. He saw the fear, anger, and humiliation over and over again in the faces of those captured and shipped off to the auction block. The agony and injustice of his race's condition was deeply imprinted on him and relegated to a hidden place in his memory—at least for the time being.

Following the American Revolution imports of slaves to North America temporarily declined as new laws prohibited and limited slavery's spread in the northern and southern states. In 1783 Captain Vesey decided to give up the slave trade, and he settled in Charleston, South Carolina, the fourth-largest city in America at the time. He decided to open a ship's chandlery, selling nautical supplies to the boat captains plying the Lowcountry rivers and enhancing the burgeoning trans-Atlantic traffic.

His slave, Denmark, was now a part of Vesey's household, performing both domestic and mercantile tasks. Unlike their counterparts on the rural plantations, skilled urban slaves enjoyed a greater freedom to move about and often were hired out by their owners for wages. Denmark was allowed to keep a small percentage of his wages as an allowance. He became a skilled carpenter and was frequently employed throughout the city as it began to rebuild after the war years. He also used his relative independence to keep up with current events by reading newspapers and absorbing conversations of city dwellers expressing opinions on the issues of the day. When Denmark won the lottery, he hoped that Joseph Vesey would see the wisdom in freeing *himself* from the job of supervising a slave.

Carefully counting out $600 from his winnings, Denmark paid Captain Vesey for his freedom on the last day of 1799. He set up a successful carpentry shop and began his life interacting among the free blacks in Charleston. (Fifty-eight percent of Charleston's total population was composed of blacks, both slaves and freedmen, by 1820.) But he never forgot the plight of his enslaved brothers. Sadly his wife and children also remained enslaved in another household so that he saw them only at the benevolence of their master.

Denmark sought every opportunity to engage others in debate about the evils of slavery. He became a member of the Hampstead African Methodist Episcopal (A.M.E.) Church, founded by Bishop Morris Brown, another free black leader mistrusted by the white community. In spite of severe restrictions on black church congregations, several thousand blacks joined A.M.E. churches throughout Charleston, and secret meetings were held extolling salvation and freedom. Vesey himself often quoted the Bible, the Declaration of Independence, and contemporary congressional debates in his impassioned arguments for the abolishment of slavery. He took inspiration from the successful slave uprising against the French in St. Domingue, which ended slavery and set up a new republic called Haiti in 1804.

In late 1821 authorities shut down the Hampstead A.M.E. Church on suspicion of antislavery activities. Outraged at this action, Denmark began planning the outline of his revolt. First, they would raid the city's arsenals, largely left unguarded at night, in a surprise attack at midnight. The weapons would be distributed to thousands of recruited slaves who would kill every white man, woman, and child, as well as blacks siding with them. Then some of the victorious rebels would sail to Haiti before any white troops could arrive to subdue them.

To implement his plot Vesey selected trusted "lieutenants" who could recruit large numbers of blacks and lead them through the completion of their bloody operations during the uprising. Among these were Peter Poyas, a ship's carpenter and strong organizer, and Jack Pritchard, known as "Gullah Jack," a conjurer who practiced traditional African magical arts and had a loyal following.

Rolla and Ned Bennett, trusted slaves in Governor Thomas Bennett's household, were invaluable in the effort to gather information on political and social events in Charleston from the white community. Monday Gell, a harness maker in his owner's livery stable, could assist in acquiring horses for the rebels' use. Other members of his core group were free blacks, sailors, and skilled craftsmen. By some accounts his army of slaves eventually grew to some 9,000 men.

Denmark was careful not to involve any slaves that were house servants, often more loyal to their masters, who might either intentionally or accidentally divulge the scheme within their household. He also took precautions that none of the leaders knew all the details of the rebellion but only their specific part of the plan. Recruits also knew only their individual leader's name and were given no more than a vague idea of what their role would be. In this way it was hoped that no one person could endanger the success of the whole plot by revealing names and detailed information.

The summer months saw an exodus of many of Charleston's white residents to cooler climates for relief from the heat and accompanying fevers. This meant an increase in the dominance of the black population in the city. Thus, Sunday, July 14, 1822, was selected as the target date for the revolt.

But the careful planning was betrayed. One of Vesey's lieutenants invited Peter Desverneys, a house servant of Col. John C. Prioleau, to join in the band of rebels. Desverneys, one of the loyal domestic slaves, was alarmed by what he heard and reported the rumor of the conspiracy to his master. The leaders he implicated were immediately arrested, but they handled themselves with such composure upon interrogation that they were released, if still kept under surveillance. The authorities continued to search for more evidence but turned up nothing of substance.

Vesey, now apprehensive, moved up the date of the revolt to Sunday, June 16. But fear had spread among the ranks, and several days before the rescheduled raid, more arrests occurred. The plot was revealed, and Vesey was identified as the instigator. Governor Bennett called up hundreds of troops to secure the city. Vesey frantically dispatched a messenger to the countryside to call in his recruits and launch the attack, but the messenger was stopped by a patrol, never reaching his destination. The element of surprise was gone, and his rebellion was vanquished.

Vesey and the other leaders were captured on June 23, and a special tribunal convened to contemplate charges against 131 blacks over the next five weeks. Thirty-eight of these were released due to insufficient evidence, but ninety-three stood trial. Of the ninety-three, sixty-seven persons were convicted in the conspiracy and twenty-six were acquitted, but eleven of these were considered so dangerous that they were transported out of the state. Thirty-five of the core group, including Vesey, Ned and Rolla Bennett, Gullah Jack, and Peter Poyas were hanged in early July 1822, with several of the bodies left dangling for days as a warning to blacks and as reassurance to Charleston's white populace. Poyas is said to have called out to his fellow conspirators from the gallows, "Do not open your lips! Die silent, as you shall see me do."

Following an eloquent entreaty of his innocence from Vesey, the judge delivered these words at his sentencing, "It is difficult to imagine what infatuation could have prompted you to attempt an enterprise so wild and visionary. You were a free man; you were comparatively wealthy; and enjoyed every comfort, compatible with your situation. You had, therefore, much to risk, and little to gain . . ."

At first what one historian called "the most elaborate and well-planned slave insurrection in the history of the United States" was intentionally erased from the fearful slave-holding public's consciousness. This insurrection in the predominantly black state of South Carolina was too well organized, too widespread, and involved too large a number of trusted slaves— simply too terrifying—to be believed or acknowledged. But though it was obscured from written records prior to the Civil War, the buried rebellion contributed to the polarization of the country on emancipation and exacerbated the socioeconomic differences in the North and the South. Perhaps Denmark Vesey's "infatuation" was an early catalyst for change and gain in the lives of future generations of black Americans.

The Other "Carolina Gold"

· 1827 ·

The water rushing through the sluice beside the gristmill outside Kershaw, South Carolina, in the winter of 1827 was especially cold. The men panning for gold in the silt hardly noticed the pain in their aching knuckles. It wasn't the same "gold fever" that caused a stampede of prospectors to rush westward into California two decades later, but it was South Carolina's gold rush just the same. And it spawned get-rich-quick dreams in the hearts of many a man.

For the next couple of years, the gold seekers washed the banks and bottoms of the mill creek on property owned by Col. Benjamin Haile, with some success. The gold found on his Lancaster County plantation was no fluke.

Excited prospectors made similar discoveries, and claims were filed in fifteen other counties across the state, with York County leading the rush having more claims than any of the rest. Other "golden" counties were Union, Edgefield, Oconee, Kershaw, Saluda, Cherokee, Abbeville, Anderson, Laurens, Newberry, Greenville, Spartanburg, and Pickens. Many of these claims never got beyond the filing stage, but a few got lucky. At one time or another, more than one hundred mines were operating in South Carolina, and as early as the 1830s, the "fever" was paying off economically, as gold mining had become the second-largest industry after agriculture.

The Haile Gold Mine provides a rich background for the story of gold mining in the state. Haile's eager workers soon found the surface gold discovered by panning played out. Deeper excavations proved more promising and led to a more concerted effort to mine the gold. In 1829 the first shipment was sent to the U.S. Mint in Philadelphia, marking the first domestic gold to come from South Carolina. One record notes the gold production of that year valued at $3,500. Anticipating significant gold yield, a Frenchman named Cugnat built a 5 Stamp Mill (a measure of production capacity) on the property in 1837, only the second stamp mill operating in the country at that time.

Extracting the gold at Haile Mine was not an easy process. Miners had to dig deeper and deeper into the ground to find traces of the ore. The gold did not appear as large, pure veins but rather as minuscule particles within the hard rock. The difficulties of this work, along with the lure of the California gold rush promising easier, quicker wealth, gradually led to abandonment of the Haile mining operations in the 1850s.

The shutdown was short-lived though because war intervened. From 1860 to 1865 the Confederacy reopened the mine to acquire mineral deposits necessary for their war materiel. The Confederates successfully obtained copperas and other chemicals from pyrite ore deposits until the Federals put an end to these endeavors on their march through the South. Arriving in Lancaster County in February 1865, General Sherman's troops, searching for treasure, took two local men prisoner, hoping to force them to reveal the location of stores of gold. They were unsuccessful in their efforts but did succeed in burning and destroying the buildings and equipment of the mine as well as much of the surrounding countryside. This devastation forced another, if more abrupt, closing of the Haile Mine.

Ownership of the property changed hands from the Haile family to James Eldridge in 1866, but operations did not resume again until 1880, when a New York group took over. They erected a 20 Stamp Mill for large-scale production. Making a profit on the yield from the rock remained a challenge for many more years in spite of new mining experiments and innovations. Just as they were about to give up on their efforts, the group hired a German mining engineer, Dr. Adolph Thies, who was anxious to try a new idea. He developed a special process to recover gold from sulfides that came to be known as the Thies Barrel Chlorination Process. Finally, the key to unlocking the gold in the hard rock was found, and the Haile Gold Mine prospered.

The leading metallurgical and mining engineers of the day came to Kershaw to study the workings of the mine as a model for mining gold through Thies's new separation process. Many improvements were made to the mill plant as the mining activity thrived. Capacity was increased to a 60 Stamp Mill, employing some 175 workers. Geologic surveys and diamond drilling were conducted, and a narrow-gauge railroad was built to haul the cars laden with ore from the mine to the mill. By the turn of the century, the Haile Gold Mine was the most famous and successful producer of gold east of the Mississippi River.

This exciting period fostered a community life for the workers that may have been typical for a gold-mining town in the rural South in its time. One former worker's memories are chronicled in the book *Death of a Gold Mine*, by Clyde Pittman. Pittman describes parties, teas, picnics, fish fries, and dances. There was a school and a chapel with "a preacher who came around once in awhile." Occasionally, "a 'sin shouter' would stage a great 'Revival'" at a tent meeting lasting several nights. The ladies of the community even formed a Literary Guild that the author suspected focused their discussions mainly on "just gossip." The center of activity was the big company store that contained a post office and the mine's office. On monthly paydays a red flag was hung out of the window, notifying workers to come collect their wages, which averaged around $1.35 per day. One dollar was withheld each month to cover the pay of the company doctor who tended to the medical care of the employees.

In comparing the rowdier side of life at Haile Mine to the lore of the camps of the Colorado or California mines, Pittman sets the scene:

> It is true that we did not have the swinging door saloon or the dance hall girls, but . . . Whiskey flowed. There were no Cowboys or gunmen with their Colt 45's tied down to their legs swaggering about, but most everyone at the Mine "packed a weapon.". . . Unlike the California gold camps we had no Chinese Coolies, but there was quite an abundance of Black laborers who flocked to the Mine in large numbers. . . . There was considerable sporting blood. . . . Dice, poker, card games of every kind flourished. . . . A foot race, chicken fight, any game of skill or chance . . . [had] plenty of backers . . . [and] fist fights and common brawling were quite ordinary.

Amazingly, order was maintained, however, with no policeman or jail, with only the intimidating appearance of a sheriff from time to time.

Turn-of-the-century camp life was bound to produce some eccentric characters, and Haile Gold Mine could claim quite a few. One that stood out was a black man named Frank Pearson, the resident fortune teller. He was feared and ridiculed by some and admired by others for his predictions based on coffee grounds and palm readings. Repeatedly he warned that a great day of judgment was coming to the Haile Mine "when this Sodom and Gomorrah will sink into a mine shaft. . . . This den of evil will be no more." His warnings proved to be grimly accurate when a great explosion took place on the morning of August 10, 1908.

A large steam boiler operating crushing equipment in the

mill blew up, completely destroying the building. Four men were seriously injured by falling brick, timbers, debris, and escaping steam. One of these was the mine manager, Ernest A. Thies (son of the inventive engineer Dr. Adolph Thies), who died the next day. "Cap'n Thies," as he was respectfully called, was greatly mourned by the workers when they lost their leader and friend. This catastrophe ended another chapter in the history of the Haile Mine. Without the leadership of Ernest Thies, the now elderly backers in New York discontinued operations.

New owners directed some intermittent work until 1917. At that time sulphur used for the World War I war effort instigated a brief period of mining activity. As the result of rising gold prices in the 1930s, the mine again resumed regular operations from 1934 to 1942, producing an estimated $2-million worth of gold. One estimate totals a lifetime production value by 1942 of $6.5 million at an average price of $35 per ounce. During World War II President Roosevelt suspended gold mining in order to direct workers to base-metal production in support of this latest war effort.

After the war, like most of the mines in the eastern United States, the Haile Mine did not reopen due to cost-prohibitive expense for reinstalling workers and equipment. It lay vacant until the mid-1970s, when the anticipation of rising gold prices interested another prospector. The Cyprus Mines briefly attempted production until prices plummeted again in 1977. In the mid-1980s, with gold selling at $320 per ounce, the Piedmont Mining Company of Charlotte, North Carolina, resumed operations on a small scale. They mined another 86,000 ounces of gold from the Haile over the next seven years. In 1992 they entered into a joint venture with Amax Gold Company of Golden, Colorado, for additional financial backing and expertise.

For now the mine is closed once more, with only occasional exploratory work. "Carolina Gold" is a phrase heavy laden with meaning for nineteenth-century South Carolinians who were part of the most exciting years of the highly profitable rice industry. But the men of the Haile Mine had a "Carolina Gold" all their own. For a time it was get rich quick, but all too soon it was over. Technology continues to evolve. Mining innovations yet unknown may hold the promise of untold wealth. Perhaps, the Haile and South Carolina's other gold mines merely lay waiting for the next epidemic of "Carolina Gold" fever to strike.

The Journey of the
Best Friend
· 1830 ·

In the 1820s America was beginning to feel its oats. The dangerous revolution for independence from England was a quarter century in the past, and this noble experiment in democracy seemed to be working. With the early stirrings of an industrial revolution on the horizon, there seemed to be nothing ahead for American society but growth and greater success. Gaining access to this endless bounty was the only problem.

As the small colonial workshops of New England were turning into manufacturing centers, they faced an increasing need for some reliable means of distribution for these goods. Canals were built, but they were slow, expensive to dig, and difficult to maintain. As the population grew, the promise of cheap, fertile lands in the West was pulling settlers away from the established population centers in the East. Homesteaders needed some means of transportation to access these new lands and send their crops back to eastern markets. The few trails that had become legitimate roads were slow and impassable in bad weather.

In the South, particularly in Georgia and South Carolina, the economic system remained agrarian, tied to the relatively cheap labor of slavery. Still, port cities like Charleston and Savannah were losing trade to the newer settlements on the western frontier. Steamboats and barges plied the southern rivers and larger navigable streams as far as they went. But these geographic limitations prevented coastal Southerners from keeping up with America's rapid growth and the economy's ravenous appetite for western expansion.

In particular, the port of Charleston, a major center of trade in colonial times, was quickly fading behind the neighboring port of Savannah. Charleston had the Santee Canal, but that was only good for flatboats moving at a snail's pace. The Savannah River, on the other hand, could handle steamboats, and its waters extended inland as far as Hamburg, South Carolina, and neighboring Augusta, Georgia.

Charleston's city fathers searched for another way to connect their port to the state's developing interior. They were vaguely aware of experiments conducted in England with an invention, yet unproven, which operated over something called a "rail road." The invention was something called a "locomotive." In 1827 news of this invention's potential reached South Carolina's General Assembly, and a petition to survey for such a "rail road" from Charleston to Hamburg was submitted. The petition was denied, but the state went out on a limb so far as to allow a corporation to be formed for that purpose. It was to be called the South Carolina Canal and Rail Road Company. "Canal" appeared in the name because Charlestonians, distrustful of the whole rail road idea, also hoped a canal could be dug between the Ashley and Savannah Rivers—just in case. The act passed on December 19, 1827.

The new company was authorized to sell stock at $100 per share, and when $700,000 was raised, construction could begin. By March of 1828 the first survey for a suitable route began. The company hired the services of Mr. Horatio Allen to be chief engineer. Mr. Allen had traveled to England, where he had actually seen the operation of the locomotive with his own eyes. There, he'd counseled with the builders of England's experimental Stockton and Darlington Railway. Allen's proposed route would run from Charleston to Hamburg—a fantastic-sounding distance of 135 miles. If they could actually build it, this would be the longest railroad in the world.

As construction started, there was general enthusiasm from South Carolinians at both ends of the line and along much of the planned right-of-way. Some property owners offered their land to the company free of charge. Other benefactors offered their slaves as labor for rail construction and grading.

Several construction methods were tried for building the rail line. What worked in the end was a pair of iron bars, 2½ inches wide and ½ inch thick, spiked to the top of wooden rails set on pilings. Even as the rails were being laid, the decision on a means of locomotion was by no means set.

The use of steam was little understood, and alternative theories about how this vehicle might be powered were explored. Not the least of these was the tried-and-true power of the wind. On March 20, 1830, a four-wheeled cart equipped with a sail was set atop the tracks near the Line Street terminus of the rail line on Charleston's upper peninsula.

According to the account published in the *Charleston Courier*, "Fifteen gentlemen got on board and flew off at the rate of 12 to 15 miles an hour." Not far up the track, "The mast went by the board with the sail and rigging attached, carrying with them several of the crew." While this experiment was cause for great sport and general amusement among the crowd of observers, the company's management never seriously considered the idea of wind power.

They did, however, seriously consider another power source—the horse. A car was actually built that employed a horse walking on a treadmill, propelling the vehicle through a series of gears connected to the axles. It was dubbed the "Flying Dutchman." Finally, Mr. Allen managed to convince the investors of that idea's folly. "In the future," he said, "there is no reason to expect any material improvements in the breed of horses," and ultimately the steam locomotive was adopted as the best viable power source for passenger and freight transportation by rail.

In the summer of 1830, construction of the first locomotive for the South Carolina Canal and Rail Road Company began. Actually manufactured in New York City and shipped to Charleston in pieces by boat, the primitive-looking contraption was named the *Best Friend* by ever-hopeful local investors and the merchants who were anxious to see it succeed.

In October the six horsepower, three-ton engine arrived and was reassembled by a team of Charleston machinists and engineers. On November 2 it was ready for a trial run. Alas, the iron wheels proved too weak to handle the lateral strain as the heavy locomotive rounded curves, so they had to be replaced with new wheels of a stronger design. This was done, and another test run was made on December 9. Then, and in subsequent trials over the next few days, the smoke-belching locomotive proved capable of speeds from 16 to 21 miles per hour, pulling four or five cars holding forty or fifty passengers. With the engine running light, it actually ran 35 miles per hour on a straight and level stretch of track!

On Christmas day of 1830, the *Best Friend of Charleston* formally made its debut in a scheduled run along the tracks that had been laid to date. The route ran from Line Street on the Charleston peninsula to the junction of State and Dorchester Roads, a distance of 6 whole miles. The locomotive was attached to two "pleasure cars" filled with excited passengers. The *Charleston Courier* breathlessly recounted the event:

> The one hundred and forty one persons flew on the wings of the wind at the speed of fifteen to twenty-five miles per hour, annihilating time and space . . . leaving all the world behind. On the return we reached Sans-Souci in quick and double quick time, stopped to take up a recruiting party—darted forth like a live rocket, scattering sparks and flames on either side—passed over three salt water creeks hop, step and jump, and landed us all safe at the

lines before any of us had time to determine whether or not it was prudent to be scared.

As a band of musicians enlivened the scene and "great hilarity and good humor prevailed throughout the day," the *Best Friend of Charleston* proved that steam locomotion on rails carried the future of American commerce.

From this point forward the success of the railroad in America was guaranteed. The hill yet to climb in terms of technology would be steep and expensive, but the road ahead led to unimaginable success and untold riches. The future of the *Best Friend,* however, was not so bright.

Just six months into the railroad's operation, on June 17, 1831, the train was idle at one of its stops while crew members resupplied the lumber car. The boiler held a full head of steam at the time, and the escape valve was hissing loudly under the summer sun. Annoyed by the irritating noise, the engineer instructed his slave to tie off the valve with his handkerchief and fix the nagging problem. In due course the mounting pressure caused the boiler to explode, killing the poor fireman and badly scalding the engineer.

This setback was only a temporary hurdle in the continuing progress of the railroad. Pieces of the *Best Friend* were soon gathered up, recycled, and rebuilt as a new locomotive called the *Phoenix,* with a few technological improvements. It and a number of other engines came along in rapid progression, each one adding to the efficiency and safety of steam locomotion by rail. It wasn't until the fall of 1833 that the entire line from Charleston to Hamburg, South Carolina, was completed, running the full length of 136 miles. Still, the brief journey of the *Best Friend* marked the onset of America's first regularly scheduled passenger and freight rail service—and it happened in South Carolina.

Mary Chesnut: Witness to War

· 1861 ·

I do not pretend to go to sleep. How can I? If Anderson does not accept terms at four o'clock, the orders are he shall be fired upon. I count four by St. Michael's chimes, and I begin to hope.

At half past four, the heavy booming of a cannon! I sprang out of bed and on my knees, prostrate, I prayed as I never prayed before.

There was a sound of stir all over the house, a pattering of feet in the corridor. All seemed to be hurrying one way. I put on my double-gown and a shawl and went to the house top. The shells were bursting . . . I knew my husband was rowing about in a boat somewhere in that dark bay, and that the shells were roofing it over, bursting toward the Fort. If Anderson were obstinate, Mr. Chesnut was to order the Forts on our side to open fire. Certainly fire had begun. The regular roar of the cannon, there it was! And who could tell what each volley accomplished of death and destruction.

The women were wild, there on the house top. Prayers from the women and imprecations from the men; and then a shell would light up the scene.

It is April 12, 1861. Mary Boykin Chesnut was staying at the Planter's Hotel in Charleston, having accompanied her husband, James Chesnut Jr. to the "City by the Sea," the hotbed of the sectional crisis. James was a member of Confederate General Pierre G. T. Beauregard's staff involved in the negotiations with Union commander Maj. Robert Anderson, occupying Fort Sumter in Charleston Harbor. Mary was an eyewitness to the unfolding drama, simultaneously feeling fear and excitement, as she well understood the ramifications of this terrible violence.

"We watched up there, and everybody wondered why Fort Sumter did not fire a shot," Mary added, but the Confederate bombardment continued until the following afternoon when Anderson surrendered the fort, now engulfed in flames. Miraculously, no lives were lost, and the South was jubilant in its expedient victory. All believed that the war would soon end.

Of course, the divisive conflict did not end soon, nor would it take place without tremendous loss of life on both sides. Mary Boykin Miller Chesnut continued to record her observations, thoughts, and experiences throughout the days of the Southern Confederacy. Mary's life was both typical and, at the same time, atypical for a member of the antebellum Southern aristocracy. She was the daughter of South Carolina Governor Stephen Decatur Miller and Mary Boykin Miller, who raised her with all the advantages of wealth and social position. She received a thorough education both in Camden near the family plantation and at an exclusive boarding school in Charleston. In addition to acquiring the social graces befitting the elite planter class, she was taught to speak fluent French and German and received intensive instruction in the classics, history, and religion. She married into another prominent family, the Chesnuts of Mulberry Plantation, located just a few miles south of Camden, where she led a pampered life largely made possible by the work of plantation slaves.

Mary was not so typical, however, regarding her viewpoints on slavery, which she vehemently opposed. And she felt just as strongly about marriage, which she considered virtually the same as slavery for women. She read voraciously, devouring literature and history, as well as current events in the newspapers and periodicals of the day. Her education, keen wit, intelligence, grace, and strength prepared her for a role she would embrace and ambitiously pursue during the war. As the wife of a Confederate general serving as advisor to President Jefferson Davis, she would follow firsthand the rise, short life, and demise of the Confederacy from the first shots at Fort Sumter, the formation of a government in Montgomery, Alabama, and the workings of the capital in Richmond, Virginia, to a bitter end back in her home state of South Carolina. "It was a way I had, always to stumble on the real show."

Mary Boykin Chesnut found herself in an extraordinary position, often surrounded by the leadership of the South at important occasions where she more than held her own, impressing generals and politicians with her knowledge of military and governmental matters. Denied any position of authority as a woman, she sought advancement for her husband, fostering his career and accompanying him to live in the places that took center stage in the drama of the Confederate nation. Plantation life was too remote and dull to suit her, and her love of social occasions thrived even in the settings of these final days of the Old South. At times her active social life created tension between Mary and James, who was more reserved and somber, but her eagerness for stimulating conversation, knowledge, and people usually won out. Fortunately, she also directed this fervor into compiling her journals, insightfully describing the major players who shaped the events of this turbulent time.

Perhaps her writings at the end of the war convey the desperation, pessimism, and depression felt by many Southerners. Upon the death of his mother, James returned with Mary to the

Chesnut home near Camden, where James was made responsible for organizing and commanding the South Carolina reserves.

At this stage of the war, the outlook was grim for the South, and the Yankees launched a double offensive to bring final defeat to the Rebels. Union generals Ulysses S. Grant and William T. Sherman took on Confederate leaders Robert E. Lee and Joseph Johnston in Virginia and Georgia in May 1864. The armies experienced heavy casualties on both sides in these engagements, but after four years of war, the South was running out of reinforcements, munitions and supplies at a much faster pace. By the end of the summer, Atlanta fell to the Federals, and an inevitable fatalism gripped the Southern people. Fully comprehending the gravity of the situation, Mary expressed her gloom as "flocks of buzzards swirling round—swooping down—flapping their nasty wings—crowding in a black cloud to pick the carcass of the dead Confederacy."

By November General Sherman had embarked on his "March to the Sea," burning and plundering his way through Georgia. With the beginning of the new year, Sherman and his troops left Savannah, turning back north with the goal of inflicting even greater destruction on the people of the Palmetto State, the instigators of secession and armed rebellion.

Once again Mary happened to be on the scene of great drama. Residing in Columbia while James struggled to muster his evaporating South Carolina reserve units, she learned of Sherman's advance on the city. James wrote her to return to Mulberry, 40 miles away, but she feared for her safety anywhere within the boundaries of her native state, the target of Northern retribution. Along with thousands of other women, Mary Chesnut became a refugee from the invading Federal troops. She decided to head north through Chester, South Carolina, crossing into North Carolina and on to Charlotte and Lincolnton. Her words revealed her plight: "I am broken-hearted, an exile." Enduring difficult and erratic train travel amidst the chaos, lack of food and decent accommodations, she described her state, "Shame, disgrace, beggary, all at once. They are hard to bear." And after learning of the burning of Columbia, more despair, "What is the good of being here at all? Our world has gone to destruction." Following the surrender she was reunited with her husband and returned to Mulberry, where the reality of starting over in a broken, unfamiliar world set in. "It is a wearisome thought; that late in life we are to begin anew, with laborious, difficult days ahead."

In the midst of coping with rebuilding their lives after the war, Mary managed to carve out time to revise and rework her journals in the hopes of their eventual publication. She did not live to see them in print, but her words live on in several edited versions of her forty-eight copybooks, which contained more than 2,500 pages. The first one is titled *A Diary from Dixie*, published in 1905, nineteen years after her death. They are an important source for historians, revealing a woman's personal experience during the Civil War. One biographer, Elisabeth Muhlenfeld, calls Mary's writings "in many respects the most remarkable first hand account of the Confederacy ever written."

For all of us, South Carolinian Mary Chesnut's diaries vividly bring to life the whirlwind of the conflict from those very first shots witnessed on the rooftop to the collapse of the antebellum South and the dramatic altercation of lives—black and white, wealthy and poor—through sweeping social, political, and economic change. Her vibrant, witty, outspoken, and human voice beseeches us to contemplate the passion and tragedy of her extraordinary times.

Penn Center, Island of Opportunity

· 1862 ·

Once the first artillery shell exploded over Fort Sumter and the opening shots of the Civil War had been exchanged, the fires of passion, long smoldering in the hearts of many Northern abolitionists, burst into flames as well. A few determined young women—many of them Unitarians or Quakers—were more than eager to do whatever they could to ease the plight of the Southern slaves. Some were driven by idealism and a true sense of duty; others sought opportunity for meaningful work, largely denied to women in the 1860s. But, like soldiers for enlightenment, they bravely headed south with lofty ambitions of righting the wrongs of slavery. Among the earliest of these women was Laura M. Towne. She was sent to South Carolina in April of 1862 by an abolitionist group in Philadelphia, Pennsylvania, calling itself the Freedmen's Association.

Alone and carrying only a few possessions and meager supplies, Laura stepped off the steamer onto the island of St. Helena in Beaufort County, close to where Union troops had established their first victorious stronghold in Port Royal the previous year. On this isolated, rural island were approximately 10,000 abandoned slaves, left behind when their masters fled as 12,000 Union forces landed on nearby Hilton Head Island.

Although the Emancipation Proclamation would not be

read by President Lincoln until January 1, 1863, the black population of St. Helena was essentially (if unofficially) liberated. They lacked two main ingredients for achieving self-sufficiency on their island home: education and title to their own lands. Laura Towne had come to address the first of these issues—education.

It was ironic that St. Helena Island would be her assignment for administering the first of the "remedies" for slavery, as St. Helena was where slavery had been introduced to America in 1526. The Spanish named it Punta de Santa Elena when they landed there in 1521. English planters arrived on Hilton Head Island in 1663. After their war with the Yemassee Indians ended in 1718, they were able to use nearby St. Elena for growing crops, primarily indigo. By the time of the American Revolution, "St. Helena" (as the island was now called) had been settled for 200 years. All the while, its use had been mostly agricultural. Its population was largely dominated by West Africans imported to work there as slaves.

The St. Helena that awaited Laura Towne must have looked intimidating, if not Rousseau-like in its natural beauty. In addition to the vast cotton fields that gave mute testimony to the slavery long practiced there, she witnessed a variety of animals and lush vegetation. Wild varieties of yellow jessamine, Cherokee roses, cassina berries, iris, and wisteria were growing in abundance. Palmettos and ancient live oaks were thriving along the marshes and tidal creeks, as they had for eons.

In this rich, natural, and isolated environment, St. Helena's black culture was able to remain apart from the distracting influences of other settings. Many of the islanders' West-African traditions were passed on through consecutive generations unaltered. For instance, St. Helena residents retained their distinct "Gullah" language—a uniquely altered blend of African, Native-American, Spanish, French, and English words. So did the famous Gullah basket weaving—so associated with the South Carolina Lowcountry—which originated with African tribes from the Gulf of Guinea down to the Cape of Good Hope.

Laura found her way to the abandoned house on the Oaks Plantation, which provided her first shelter. Eventually, one room of the old house served as her school. The first job, however, was serving the blacks' immediate need for medical care. As it happened, she was in a limited position to help in this capacity as well as start a school. She had been educated at the Women's Medical College in Philadelphia, and her training helped her quickly become the island's "doctor." She dispensed medical care as best she could and served as a midwife while setting up classes for her school.

The enormity of the task must have been overwhelming. She wrote back to the Freedmen's Association in Pennsylvania asking for help, and the following June another teacher, a Canadian-born Quaker named Ellen Murray, arrived. A third teacher, Charlotte Forten, was an African American from Salem, Massachusetts, who arrived in October that same year. Only the diaries of Charlotte Forten and Laura Towne survive as records of the first years of what is known as "the Port Royal Experiment." Miss Forten left after the first year due to ill health, but Miss Towne and Miss Murray stayed on for the next forty years of their lives.

The women called their school "Penn Normal" in honor of William Penn and their home state. Their students were a mix of ex-slaves and their descendants, refugees of war, and a few African captives who had been brought to America just before the start of the war.

Part of the success of the Penn Normal School may have stemmed from the fact that much of the Civil War's calamity and disruption took place "offstage" from St. Helena Island. Even while hostilities with Northern troops continued on the mainland, the black community on St. Helena was largely self-governing. After freedom was finally theirs, life changed very little on St. Helena. The exception was the issue of land ownership.

One of the first orders issued by Gen. William Tecumseh

Sherman in preparation for Reconstruction was Special Field Order No. 15, which appropriated the South Carolina sea islands for use by freed slaves. He assigned Gen. Rufus Saxon the formidable task of identifying the head of each black household and assigning each of these men "forty acres of land and the temporary use of a military horse or mule."

St. Helena's blacks continued living on the land as they had before—working the same fields some of their ancestors had worked as slaves—only now *they* were the landowners. Even through the end of the nineteenth century, most of the landholders on St. Helena were the grown children or the grandchildren of former slaves who originally had been granted land by the newly victorious Federal Government.

Laura found the blacks on St. Helena to be eager learners. School enrollment quickly outgrew the one-room space allocated in the old plantation house. They moved into the island's brick Baptist Church, which had been built by slave labor back in 1855. But soon that space was too small as well. Miss Towne purchased land, and an early version of a prefabricated school building was sent to South Carolina by the Philadelphia-based sponsors. The unassembled building was shipped all the way to Beaufort by boat.

Although the school was a great success, the money from the Freedmen's Association soon ran out. Miss Towne was forced to pay the other teachers from her own meager salary, but the school struggled on despite the hardship. When Miss Towne's health began to fail in 1900, help arrived in the personage of Mr. P. W. Dawkings, a follower of Booker T. Washington and a man generally considered to be a leading authority in African-American education. After Miss Towne's death in 1901, he became Superintendent of Industries at Penn Normal and organized the islanders into farmer's "conferences," like those he'd seen at Tuskegee Institute. Self-reliance was the key, he emphasized. He also instituted a school farm and opened the door for industrial education at Penn.

Carpentry, blacksmithing, wheel wrighting, basket weaving, harness making, cobbling, and mechanics followed suit. By 1909 a full-time agricultural instructor was on the faculty, and the school adopted the name Penn Normal Industrial and Agricultural School. Graduates had the option of continuing their schooling to become teachers, and many went on to work in the county schools scattered throughout the sea islands.

For the most part these small-scale but successful farmers were spared the closed economic cycle called "sharecropping," which bound generations of Southern blacks to poverty. They were also spared the political and societal insult of segregation, as the blacks had always been in the vast majority on the island. What they lacked economically they made up for with the confidence that came from owning their own land. Whites—and their Southern segregation—stayed away from St. Helena, as it was believed to be too swampy and malarial for safe habitation. The Southern culture played out its story into the twentieth century without much participation from St. Helena, even though it was the largest of Beaufort County's sixty-five separate islands.

In 1948 Beaufort County finally took over the financial responsibility of education on St. Helena Island. Classes at Penn continued until a public school was built. The last graduates from Penn Center received their diplomas in 1958.

During the 1950s and early 1960s, Penn's campus became a major retreat for civil-rights groups headed by Dr. Martin Luther King Jr. During the early 1960s Dr. King and his staff met there often to plan strategies for social change. Not the least of these planning sessions resulted in the March on Washington, D.C., in 1963. A private retreat for Dr. King was built on St. Helena, but the leader was assassinated in Memphis, Tennessee, in 1968 before he had the opportunity to stay there.

Over the years the school's role as a catalyst for self-reliance has become a beacon of hope for generations of black South Carolinians. Penn Center, as it is now known, is a conference center for educational, religious, and cultural development used by students and scholars from all over America. Penn Center was designated as one of South Carolina's three National Historic Landmark Districts in 1974.

Robert Smalls: The Gullah Statesman

· 1875 ·

In the early morning hours of May 13, 1862, a twenty-three-year-old steamer pilot named Robert Smalls carefully steered a Confederate transport vessel, bristling with armaments, out of Charleston Harbor. Among its other precious cargo, the 150-foot *Planter* was also carrying Smalls's wife and children plus twelve other passengers. Like many men who piloted craft through Charleston Harbor, Smalls had extensive knowledge of its waters and the defenses associated with its blockade. But Robert Smalls was no ordinary steamer pilot—he was a slave.

At the age of twelve Robert had come to Charleston from the small, coastal town of Beaufort, South Carolina, where his mother was a slave in the home of the McKee family. Although Robert and his mother lived in relative comfort as house servants, on trips to the neighboring plantations he witnessed the cramped living quarters, sparse food, long hours of strenuous labor, and often-severe punishments. This aspect of slavery influenced his thinking both as a young adult and throughout the course of his life, fueling his sense of injustice at the plight of the Negro in the antebellum South.

Charleston was a beautiful, bustling, and prosperous city, largely built by the labor of skilled black artisans and craftsmen. There Robert was employed (with all wages handed over to his master) in a series of jobs including waiter and lamplighter for the city. As a young man, he found work as a stevedore, loading onto northern ships one of the main export crops of the area, Sea Island cotton. At the John Simmons Shipyard, he became an expert rigger, absorbing much knowledge about the waterfront. He studied charts, channels, currents, and tides, noting the locations of shoals and reefs in Charleston Harbor. By the outbreak of the Civil War, he had acquired an extensive mastery of the waters along the South Carolina and Georgia coasts. Smalls paid his owner $15 a month to hire himself out for work. In July 1861 the Confederates hired him as a deckhand on the former cotton steamer, *Planter*. His seamanship capabilities were soon recognized, and he attained the position of wheelsman by March 1862.

Planter had been converted earlier that year into a special dispatch boat for Gen. Roswell Ripley, in charge of the Confederate forces around Charleston. Due to its large carrying capacity, the ship transported troops and supplies to the fortifications around the city, and Smalls demonstrated his abilities in successfully handling the vessel in and out of the harbor inlets. In this trusted position as civilian pilot, he learned all the secret Confederate codes and signals for passing the harbor forts. He had even assisted in the placement of torpedo fields in Charleston waterways as part of the Confederate defenses.

Smalls had been waiting for just the right moment to commandeer the ship, filled with Rebel guns and ammunition. His audacious plan was to turn it over to the Union forces, waiting in the waters just off Charleston. If he succeeded in this daring plot, he would obtain freedom for himself and his family. But discovery of his scheme by the Confederates meant capture and certain death for all.

It's difficult to imagine Smalls's state of mind as he slipped under the guns of the Rebel forts. He gave each lookout the correct whistle signal as he passed and knew that the closest Union blockade ship, *Onward*, was already preparing to fire on the approaching Confederate vessel. With what must have been a combination of fear and determined resolve, he brought the *Planter,* flying a white flag of surrender, alongside the *Onward.*

Lifting a captain's broad-brimmed hat in the air, Smalls is said to have called out "Good Morning, Sir! I have brought you some of the old United States' guns, Sir!"

This bold and courageous maneuver delivering the *Planter* into Union hands immediately garnered Smalls national acclaim as a Union hero; overnight, he was a media sensation. Northern newspapers pronounced him the "First Hero of the Civil War." Smalls and his crew were praised as the "plucky Africans" for presenting the Union blockade with "the first trophy from Fort Sumter."

Beyond the symbolism of his daring deed, Smalls's experience was strategically invaluable. He revealed to the Union the placement of mines and Rebel troop locations and fortifications, plus he offered up a Confederate codebook. This information was relayed to Admiral DuPont, the commander of the South Atlantic Blockading Squadron. DuPont promptly retained Smalls as permanent pilot of the *Planter* and utilized his navigational talents on other vessels because of his intimate knowledge of local waters.

On May 30, 1862, President Abraham Lincoln signed a bill in Congress awarding prize money to Smalls and his accomplices. Smalls personally received $1,500 for his role in commandeering the *Planter.*

While still in service to the Union, Smalls was sent on a speaking tour by abolitionists, who recognized his ability to articulate the message of the freedmen. He was somewhat reluctant to accept the trappings of his newfound fame, but in September 1862, "the colored citizens of New York" presented him with a gold medal "as a token of our regard for his heroism, love of liberty, and his patriotism." He was also persuaded by Maj. Gen. David Hunter to help organize the 1st South Carolina Volunteers of black men (former slaves) to fight for the

Union. Smalls helped plead the cause to President Lincoln, asking for uniforms, equipment, and adequate pay. When their request was granted, Robert Smalls was witness to the power of political clout firsthand. With the war still raging, he returned to South Carolina, participating in seventeen battles by war's end.

In the spring of 1863, Smalls piloted another Union monitor, *Keokuk*, during an attack on Fort Sumter. The firing was intense, and the *Keokuk* took more than ninety hits. He was wounded in the eyes during this battle, but survived, despite the sinking of his ship the next morning. Back on the *Planter* the following December, he went on to distinguish himself for bravery. *Planter* was caught between two Confederate batteries and a Rebel ship and drew intense bombardment. While the Union captain hid belowdecks, Smalls took command of the leaderless *Planter,* bringing her to safety. The Union commander was dismissed on a charge of cowardice, and Smalls was made captain in his place. Thus he became the first African-American captain of a naval vessel in the service of the United States.

When Smalls took the *Planter* to Philadelphia for repairs, he was selected as one of the first four black men to attend a national political conclave, the Republican Convention in Baltimore. Because of his confining military responsibilities, he was unable to attend the convention but used this time in Philadelphia to learn to read and write. He also polished his speaking skills with audiences at Freedmen's Aid Societies and at abolitionist and church groups—both black and white.

Following the war Robert Smalls returned home to Beaufort with his wife and children. He used his Congressional prize money to purchase the McKee house, in which he and his mother had been slaves, at government auction.

For the rest of his life he worked through the political system to achieve his goals. Public education "open without charge to all classes of persons" was a foremost cause for Smalls. He served as the registrar of qualified voters in Beaufort

County, and he was elected as a delegate to a state convention during Reconstruction. Smalls was elected to the first General Assembly to convene under the new constitution and was present when South Carolina was formally readmitted to the Union.

Smalls went on to serve as a state representative and senator in Columbia for seven years. His ability to speak to the predominantly black population of Beaufort County in their Gullah dialect, combined with his racial pride and leadership skills, assured his reelection during the Reconstruction era. He was instrumental in finding funding for free public schools, and he spearheaded efforts to improve railroad service and construct public roads.

Smalls's experience on the Lowcountry rivers proved invaluable as he called for the regulation of pilots in the South Carolina ports and worked toward the establishment of a navy yard at Parris Island, near Beaufort. In March of 1875, when Smalls was thirty-six years old, he was elected to the Forty-fourth United States Congress, representing South Carolina's Fifth District. As he took the oath of office on the Congressional floor in December 1875, thoughts of his early life in slavery, his bold strike for freedom, his wartime service, and his role in the struggle to reconstruct the divided nation must have been in mind.

"The Gullah Statesman" continued to serve for five terms in Congress as a champion of human rights and equal opportunity for all citizens. In one of his most impassioned pleas in November 1895, he made the case against the regressive groundswell for the disfranchisement of blacks in South Carolina:

> My people need no special defense, for the past history of them in this country proves them to be the equal of any people anywhere. All they need is an equal chance in the battle of life.

The Great Shake

·1886·

Without a moment's warning, a subterranean roar was heard, buildings shook from garret to cellar, the fearful noises growing louder and louder, buildings swaying to and fro like trees in a storm, and then came the crash of tumbling houses, and simultaneously mingling with those notes of horror, came the shrieks and wailings of frightened women and children.

A staff writer for the *News and Courier,* the local Charleston newspaper, described the Great Earthquake of 1886 in his dramatic account just after the main shock on August 31, 1886. Drama and alarm notwithstanding, the property damage, injury, and death toll of the quake was the most extensive to strike the eastern United States in recorded history.

Earlier in the summer several smaller tremors had been felt in Charleston, some strong enough to rattle the window sashes of the Federal Courthouse downtown on Broad Street. The rattling was compared to the effects of a boiler explosion or the jarring created by horse-drawn wagons passing by. In Summerville, a small town 20 miles north of Charleston, these tremors were more intense, and a boomlike noise was heard there four days earlier on the morning of August 27. Then, at

4:45 A.M. on the 28th, a second shock was warily noted in both Summerville and Charleston.

The main quake occurred at 9:51 P.M. on August 31, soon after many of Charleston's residents had gone to bed for the night. The initial shake lasted for only about forty-five to fifty-five seconds, followed nine minutes later by a major, if less severe, aftershock. There were four additional, significant shocks before midnight, and three more were felt in the early hours of the next day.

Throughout the long night Charlestonians endured the breaking and shattering of their homes and businesses as walls and foundations, weakened by the shock, gave way and collapsed. The crashing of falling wood, glass, stone, brick, and mortar punctuated the blackness of the night. The only illumination evident came from scattered fires that resulted from shattered oil lamps and broken gas lines. The terror manifested itself through shrieks, cries of pain, shouts, wailing, and prayers emanating from all sections of the city. Charleston's residents could only wait breathlessly for the next shake to come and pass, hoping for the chaos to subside.

Dr. Gabriel Manigault, physician, naturalist and curator of the Charleston Museum, expressed the observations of many witnesses in this way:

> Although the [earlier] shocks at Summerville excited uneasiness in Charleston, no one was prepared for what followed. During the afternoon of August 31, between 5 o'clock and sunset, the atmosphere was unusually sultry and quiet, the breeze from the ocean that usually accompanies the rising tide was almost entirely absent, and the setting of the sun was followed by a glow which was only slightly noticeable. As the hour of 9:50 was reached, there was suddenly heard a rushing, roaring sound compared by some to a train of cars at no great distance, by others to a

clatter produced by two or more omnibuses moving at a rapid rate over a paved street; by others again to an escape of steam from a boiler. It was followed immediately by a thumping and beating of the earth underneath the houses, which rocked and swayed to and fro. Furniture was violently moved and dashed to the floor, pictures were swung from the walls and, in some cases, completely turned with their backs to the front, and every moveable thing was thrown into extraordinary convulsions. It was probably then, during the period of the greatest sway, that so many chimneys were broken off at the junction with the roof . . . The first impulse with every one, as soon as the severity of the shock was realized, was to leave the house immediately, and seek a place of safety either on the street pavement outside, or on some part of the premises at a safe distance from the risk of falling walls. There were some remarkable escapes from the falling of two piazzas, one above the other, which were detached by the rocking of the brick walls, but in a few cases persons attempting to escape were fatally injured before they could reach a safe refuge. . . . It is probable that, if the shock had occurred during the business hours of the day, the falling chimneys would have caused many more casualties.

Daylight revealed the grim reality. The city had experienced much more damage than had been suspected. Ninety percent of the city's structures were damaged, and 102 buildings were completely destroyed. Almost all of the city's 14,000 chimneys toppled over. The fires caused more severe damage in isolated locations, where twenty buildings succumbed to the flames. Mercifully, however, the winds of the seaside city were relatively calm that night, and the Charleston firemen reacted quickly so that widespread fires did not occur.

The dead and injured were carried to parks and squares, where the dazed citizens began to process the calamity. There was a general apprehension that a tidal wave might follow, at any moment submerging the entire peninsula. Hundreds of black and white families were displaced from their destroyed homes and were forced to camp in open areas of downtown city parks. Their makeshift tents were constructed of sheets, blankets, carpets, clothing, and anything else at hand. *Harper's Weekly* described the scene at Marion Square, across from the old Citadel (the state's military college), as a "City of Tents." Food was not lacking, but the means of preparing and preserving it were severely limited. One account reported an official death record of twenty-seven, with an additional eighty-three or more lives lost due to injuries and exposure. Although the number of wounded persons was high, an exact count was never determined.

Charleston was still reeling from the aftermath of the Civil War, just twenty years earlier, and the long Reconstruction era that followed. Nevertheless the city pulled together in the face of this new tragedy. Another newspaper account reported, "Thousands of blacks and whites alike—no difference was recognized and no discrimination shown—were the recipients of the bounty of their more fortunate fellow-citizens, who proved to be neighbors in the hour of misfortune."

Many residents chose to evacuate, and they visited friends and relatives away from Charleston. The railroads provided free transportation for anyone who could not pay the fare. Sailors from visiting ships in the harbor came ashore to offer assistance. Much-needed aid began to pour in from other cities around the country and even from abroad.

The 1886 value of property damage in Charleston and surrounding areas was reported at $5,500,000, the present-day equivalent of more than $75 million. A recent state study concluded that at this time, an event equal in magnitude to the

1886 quake today would result in a $14-billion statewide damage cost. Seismological instrumentation was not yet developed when Charleston shook in 1886, but contemporary studies, based on the extent of the structural damage to the buildings in Charleston and the radius of the tremors spreading out from the historic city, have led to an estimate of between 6.8 and 7.7 on the Richter scale. Most estimates record the earthquake at 7.5. (American seismologist Charles Richter developed his measurement for the strength of earthquakes in 1936.)

The shock waves of the Great Shake reached far beyond the South Carolina Lowcountry. Fallen chimneys and wrecked buildings were reported upstate in Columbia. Charlotte, Asheville, and Raleigh, North Carolina were similarily affected. Extensive damage was suffered in Savannah and Augusta in Georgia, as well. Reports arrived of earthquake debris in Atlanta, but not as great as the closer cities. Tremors were felt as far away as Boston and Chicago to the north, Bermuda due east, and Cuba to the south.

Charleston's recovery from the Great Earthquake of 1886 lasted for many difficult and tiresome months. The cleaning, repairing, and rebuilding of the once-beautiful city's houses, gardens, and structures was a painstaking process as was rebuilding all the broken lives. But just as the city had done so many times before, Charleston picked up the pieces and moved forward with hope for the future. Its long history of both manmade disasters—the bombardment and siege of war—and natural occurrences—devastating fire, flood, storm, hurricane and, now, earthquake—had taught Charleston the value of resurgence. A new city arose from the rubble of the Great Shake. Charleston had survived, just as it had done over and over again throughout its 200-year-long history.

Following the earthquake federal engineers made the recommendation that "all masonry walls should be securely anchored to the floor, ceiling, and roof timbers with iron anchors built into the walls and firmly secured to the timbers."

Charlestonians took this advice to heart so that the iron rods and gib plates, commonly called "earthquake bolts," are still a ubiquitous presence on many of the city's buildings dating back to that time. In many cases the earthquake bolts have a decorative motif, such as stars and lion's heads, or they may be a simple round or cross-shaped plate. The aesthetic value of the earthquake bolts affords provenance to the structure's history. Their protective value in a major tremor, however, is still unproven—awaiting the next big test.

Mr. Roosevelt and the Pine Forest Inn

• 1889 •

Twenty crisply uniformed men on horseback anxiously awaited the guest due to arrive at 7:00 P.M. Finally they could hear, but not see in the winter darkness, the approaching train as it slowed to a halt at the depot. The men steadied their horses and readied themselves for their task of escorting the President of the United States, Theodore Roosevelt, to his lodging at the Pine Forest Inn in Summerville, South Carolina.

Once the robust president and his party with all their belongings were loaded into buggies, the caravan got underway for the short trip through the night air. Each liveried escort carried a lit torch to help guide the way along the country roads, surrounded by the now-famous towering pine trees, as they made their way to the Inn.

One of the finest moments for the Pine Forest Inn was the gala banquet held for the president and his distinguished party when they attended the South Carolina Interstate and West Indian Exposition in Charleston in 1902. The Inn's owner, Capt. F. W. Wagener, was serving as president of the Exposition Company and had successfully enticed President Roosevelt to visit both the Exposition in Charleston and his Pine Forest Inn.

As a newspaper account revealed, for the occasion the dining room "was decorated with much of the naturally beautiful foliage of the vicinity and around the hall were mounds of pine tops." One innovation for the occasion was the special dress of the waiters, who wore neckties of red, white, and blue, plus boutonnieres of miniature American flags. For the "handsome dinner," at which Captain Wagener had instructed "absolutely no expense should be spared," champagne toasts were raised to President Roosevelt's health and the united nation. The inn's "splendid orchestra" accompanied "those at the table . . . playing . . . selections [that] were particularly pleasant."

President Roosevelt was but one of the notable visitors that were coming on a regular basis to the village of Summerville. Cosmetic-industry queen Elizabeth Arden; internationally renowned violinist Efrem Zimbalist Sr. and his wife, opera singer Alma Gluck; Pulitzer Prize–winning poet Edna St. Vincent Millay; and yet another U.S. president, Howard Taft, were all drawn to the "Pineland Village" just 22 miles north of Charleston. What was the attraction of this tiny community nestled away from the mainstream of American life at the turn of the twentieth century?

It all started with the first International Tuberculosis Congress held in Paris, France, in 1889. Physicians and specialists in respiratory disorders named Summerville, South Carolina, as one of the two best locales in the world for the treatment and cure of pulmonary diseases. (The other location named was Thomasville, Georgia.) A professor from the New York Polyclinic, Dr. R. C. M. Page, advised that patients, especially those with heart complications, would benefit from "low, dry altitudes in a pine wood region, where the air is charged with derivatives of turpentine." Summerville, a town of some 3,000 people, was "just what the doctor ordered," with its bucolic, natural setting, abundance of pine trees, and mild climate. A travel brochure would later describe "the delightfully unprogressive" town situated among the "naturally pure air infused with the tonic of primeval pine" with "skillful and eminent physicians residing in the place." For generations it had enjoyed a local reputation as a healthful retreat. Now with this proclamation Summerville was thrust into the international spotlight, attracting consumptives, asthmatics, and healthy visitors alike, which boosted the community's economy practically overnight. A building boom was launched to meet the demand for lodging and services.

Among the luxury hotels and inns erected, expanded, or renovated to handle this influx of tourism, the Pine Forest Inn was one of the most elaborate. Charleston merchants F. W. and George A. Wagener built the inn and opened its doors in 1891 to the discerning needs of a sophisticated clientele. A New York architect designed the Victorian-style complex of buildings, and a local builder, Alexander J. Baird, oversaw the extensive construction project, which lasted several years. In one of the inn's early advertising brochures, the architectural style of the main building is described as "of a light fantastic character, with turrets and pinnacles in fanciful castellated style. . . . graceful graduated pyramids, ending in iron finials, rise from either end of the front roof. In the center . . . the four story structure is an upward projection on which are placed twin pyramidal towers, truncated."

Inside this impressive structure was a central rotunda, with lobbies on each floor. The entrance hall connected two large front and rear piazzas for "taking the air." Two side wings extended from the front facade, enclosing a courtyard in the rear on three sides. Wooden arches graced the interiors, dividing the spaces. The main floor contained a grand parlor with two large fireplaces, smaller ladies' private parlors, reception and reading rooms, as well as wine and smoking rooms. The dining room could seat up to 250 people, and one of the parlors, named the Rocking Chair Room to tout its main feature, was filled with more than one hundred rocking chairs. Much of the decor consisted of—what else—pine paneling and flooring, either highly polished or stained. Throughout the rotunda, main parlor, and dining room, Southern curly pine was used. The public rooms grandly displayed carved oak mantels and marble hearths.

The three upper floors featured "150 sleeping apartments," both suites and singles. Private baths and electric bells for twenty-four-hour service were among the amenities that were state of the art for the time. Almost every room contained an open fireplace that glowed with a crackling fire during the winter season, in addition to steam-radiator heat. The natural lighting from each room's windows was augmented with electric lighting provided by the Inn's own power plant. Elevators assisted those guests not electing (or able) to take the stairs. For those desiring a more private setting, five furnished "cottages" were situated on the grounds, complete with telephones linking them to the main office to summon the delivery of meals or other services. A telegraph office and long-distance telephone service kept patrons, many of whom were on extended respites for several months, in touch with their lives back home.

Top-notch chefs and German bakers prepared the finest cuisine from local produce. Fresh meats and seafood were brought in daily by train from markets in both Charleston and New York. The Pine Forest Inn also ran its own dairy, hennery, and dovecote. The inn's wells supplied both artesian (or mineral) and spring water. Dinner music was provided by professional musicians, and patrons could enjoy dancing after dinner, accompanied by an orchestra.

While the inn's seasonal guests were recuperating or just relaxing, a plethora of leisure activities and entertainment was offered about the grounds. An amusement-hall annex accommodated three bowling alleys, shuffleboard, and billiard tables. Additional outdoor pastimes included croquet and fishing. Organized activities included lawn tennis and card parties, teas, and local historical tours. One of the most popular tours was the Pinehurst Tea Garden, an experimental tea farm cultivating plants from China, Ceylon, India, and Japan. The tea farm was located near the inn and was joined to it by scenic, brick-paved walkways through a garden of hundreds of camellias, azaleas, roses, and hydrangeas, bordered by benches and gazebos that offered restful moments along the way.

For the more active guests, an array of leisure pursuits was available. In 1903 the Charleston *News and Courier* described the Pine Forest Inn as "a famous resort where far from the blasts of wintry winds hundreds of Northern and Western tourists spend happy days golfing, shooting, driving, and riding among the glorious pines." An eighteen-hole golf course "stretched for several miles" and was laid out, as the brochure described, by a "professional from the North who has played on the celebrated links of St. Andrews, Scotland." A "conveniently appointed [clubhouse] with commodious lockers [was accessible] for ladies and gentlemen." The Pine Forest Inn's golf course was the second built in South Carolina and one of the earliest in the United States.

The hunting parties found deer, opossum, raccoon, rabbit, fox, quail, dove, and wild turkey plentiful in the woodlands of a hunting preserve called Ingleside Plantation, 6 miles from town. The season lasted from the first of December to the first of April, and champion hunting dogs were provided to complete the experience if a guest did not bring his own favored hounds to the inn's kennels. The plantation's colonial-era mansion house served as a unique clubhouse for the hunters. A livery with sixty horses, as well as ponies and goats, with every type of buggy or cart was on hand for venturing out into the surrounding countryside. A staff of liverymen kept ladies' and gentlemen's saddles ready at all times, and private drivers were on constant call.

With the grand scale of the facilities, the extensive and beautifully landscaped grounds, the wide range of amenities and services, and the recreational offerings, the Pine Forest Inn may be considered one of the first resort health spas in the United States. It was clearly the leading lady among the local inns and played a vital role in the Golden Age of Summerville, a period of widespread popularity and economic prosperity, which lasted for several decades into the 1930s. Eventually the Great Depression, World War II, and an increased interest in Florida resorts led to the demise of the Inn, forcing it to close and later be torn down.

But it is fascinating to know that once upon a time the village of Summerville, South Carolina, was famous for its "curative air" and Southern hospitality. It was a chosen destination for presidents, celebrities, as well as pulmonary patients eager to regain their vitality and health. Even Teddy Roosevelt, who suffered from severe asthma as a child, was lured to this pineland village in hopes that it would enhance his presidential vigor. He was one of thousands of visitors who came for a restorative retreat from a world racing into the twentieth century.

Birth of "The Charleston"

· 1895 ·

"What these boys need is motivation," said the Reverend Daniel J. Jenkins, founder of the Charleston, South Carolina, orphanage that bore his name from 1891 to 1982. "Music is a great motivator. I think I'll start a boys band." The Jenkins Orphanage Band turned out to be not only a motivator and career catalyst for generations of homeless children, it is credited with originating the dance craze that swept the country in the 1920s—the dance now known the world over as "The Charleston."

After finding four homeless and hungry boys huddled in a stairwell of a vacant building in 1891, the Reverend Mr. Jenkins established his private institution to shelter these "lost black lambs," as he called them. By 1895 the orphanage had taken in more than 500 needy children. The musical band he formed that year was a badly needed fund-raising tool for the quickly growing orphanage as much as it was a motivator of homeless boys. But the idea was a brilliant success on both counts.

From the very beginning musical instruction at the Jenkins Orphanage was serious business. Training for the band began at age seven or eight. First, the youngsters would learn to sing their parts, and then they were given an instrument (generally used and somewhat worse for wear) and taught how to play it.

This method of instruction turned out young horn players with extraordinary skill and musicianship.

In the beginning they played sacred music, then familiar overtures, and finally popular music from the street. They played ragtime tunes, military marches, and even a little jazz. The latter came in with the runaway boys who were sent back to the orphanage with musical influences from sometimes "unusual" places. Among these influences was ethnic music from the nearby barrier islands, where old African rhythms and dances survived from pre-slavery days.

The band made its debut on the public streets of Charleston with permission granted by Charleston's mayor, police chief, and the Chamber of Commerce. For uniforms the boys wore cut-down castoffs from The Citadel, an elite southern military college then located in downtown Charleston. Visitors to the city loved to hear the boys play their brassy music and watch them show off a few fancy dance steps on street corners and in the markets. Before long crowds of people would gather and follow the band as it paraded through the streets of Charleston. One of the boys would pass a hat through the crowd while the others played, and the contributions quickly amounted to a tidy sum for the orphanage.

One of the dance steps people most enjoyed was a crazy thing—outward heel kicks combined with up-and-down movements, achieved by bending and straightening the knees in time to the syncopated 4/4 rhythm. It required loose limbs and a certain mix of skillful control and wild abandon. According to most dance historians, first mention of the dance step described as "The Charleston" appeared in print sometime around 1903. But most likely the dance (or some version of it) had been done on the streets of Charleston for quite some time.

The Jenkins Orphanage Band's jazzy, up-tempo music fostered a natural inclination to dance. The sound was practically infectious. "To hear that orphanage band was an electrifying experience," wrote one observer many years later. "Everything [about them] was perfect. The first time I heard that band I thought I had died and gone to heaven." (The Reverend Mr. Jenkins would have appreciated the religious reference.) Jenkins insisted the boys learn to read music and play with strict precision and discipline, as well as have fun.

Playing in the band required a serious commitment from every musician. The year began in May, with practice sessions that prepared the boys to "tour" outside the orphanage from June to September. In August, however, the boys had to be back in school. Eventually, these tours reached farther and farther from Charleston, and audiences grew beyond casual passers-by on street corners and impromptu parades. The band attracted a following, and concert dates were arranged. By the 1920s there were five different bands from the Jenkins Orphanage touring the United States from Florida to Maine.

When Easter came, the bands converged for group performances in New York City where some of the older boys would be recruited to play in Harlem orchestras. It is known that "The Charleston" dance step was observed in certain Harlem night spots as early as 1913, but the real breakthrough for the dance didn't come until the early 1920s.

One day in 1922, finishing touches were being given to the elaborate sets and glittering costumes for the new edition of the fabulous Ziegfeld Follies at Manhattan's New Amsterdam Theater. The show's director, Ned Wayburn—a celebrity in his own right—was overseeing every detail to ensure that this year's show would be another spectacle befitting these heady, exuberant, post–World War I days. Longtime stage veterans and friends Eubie Blake and Noble Sissle stopped by the theater to see Mr. Wayburn. They brought along a young dancer from Harlem to show the famous producer something they thought he'd want to see.

Eubie sat down at the rehearsal piano, and the boy broke into a dance Wayburn would later describe as a "gawky zest," an irresistible dance step that instantly mesmerized all onlookers.

Watching from backstage was an audience of seasoned set jockeys and sophisticated young performers who were hard to impress with anything new, especially a dance step. But as the fleet-footed kid from Harlem finished his impromptu demonstration, the theater became eerily quiet.

Wayburn asked the boy where he learned this exuberant gyration. The boy replied, "Charleston, sir. Charleston, South Carolina." And from that point on, the carefree dance that so captured the imagination of a Jazz Age generation would have a name.

Wayburn knew a potential stage hit when he saw one. He used the step in a new show he produced called *Shuffle Along,* the first all-black musical on Broadway. Two years later, the dance was featured in another show, *Runnin' Wild,* which was seen by even wider audiences. The composer for *Runnin' Wild* was James P. Johnson, a black pianist who worked with such jazz greats as "Fats" Waller and Duke Ellington. That same year, Johnson recorded a piano roll of his new hit show-stopper "Charleston" and dedicated it to the sailors working on the docks in Charleston, South Carolina.

Other songwriters soon jumped on the bandwagon, and a number of "Charleston" songs went onto records, piano rolls, and sheet music. There was "Charleston Crazy," "Original Charleston Strut," and "Just Wait Till You See My Baby Do The Charleston Dance," to name just a few. Even Louis Armstrong played something entitled "Don't Forget to Mess Around When You're Doing The Charleston." While these obscure titles are now long forgotten, they all shared that distinctive syncopated rhythm. Soon, dancers of all ages on both sides of the Atlantic were kicking and flapping and singing, "Charleston-n-n-n, Charleston-n-n-n. . . . "

Silent screen star Louise Brooks was notorious for her racy version of the dance. She epitomized "the flapper" to a generation of young Americans eager to cast off the moralistic constraints of their Victorian-era parents. When Hollywood legend

Joan Crawford was still an unknown actress struggling as a movie extra, she turned producers' heads when she danced "The Charleston" at trendy nightspots in the young film colony. And the winner of the 1925 Texas State Charleston Contest was an energetic fourteen-year-old from Fort Worth whose prize for winning was a four-week turn on the vaudeville stage. This tour and her version of the dance turned out to launch the long career of Hollywood's Ginger Rogers.

As for the Jenkins Orphanage Band, it eventually became known as a "farm" for top-quality jazz musicians. Several members of the band grew up to play in the famous orchestras of luminaries like Count Basie, Louis Armstrong, and Duke Ellington.

Was the young man from Harlem who danced for Ned Wayland in the wings of the New Amsterdam Theater back in 1922 an alumnus of the Reverend Mr. Jenkins's Orphanage band? History doesn't say. But clearly "The Charleston" made history: It captured the heart of Gertrude Stein's "Lost Generation," it was the spirit of F. Scott Fitzgerald's Jazz Age, and it wore out many a pair of shoes on the street corners and polished dance floors of its namesake city and the world.

Heigh Ho, Come to the Fair

· 1901 ·

Americans encountered a highly contagious fever of enthusiasm after the 1893 opening of the World Columbian Exposition in Chicago. After all, this (literally) electrifying peek into America's future, unveiled along the glistening waters of Lake Michigan, attracted 200,000 visitors from all across the country on its opening day alone. Awestruck newspaper wags of the day could hardly contain their exuberance for this greatest of all world's fairs. They admonished, "Sell the cook stove if you must, but come to this fair!" The gleaming "White City," as they called it, was hailed as a not-to-be missed preview of the exciting century that lay ahead for us all.

Even international critics gave the fair's organizers high praise for their ingenuity and enterprise. They claimed it opened the world's eyes to this Midwestern hub as the undiscovered crossroads of America. They said Chicago's booming economic heartbeat would set the pace for the high-stepping parade into our country's future as a great world power.

South Carolinians—still struggling against the poverty brought on by their defeat in the Civil War and smarting from the punishment of postwar Reconstruction—were hardly immune to this fever. Any kind of enthusiasm for a better tomorrow came as sweet music to Southern ears. If a world's fair, an exhibition, some kind of architectural extravaganza on a grand scale could do all that for Chicago, then this was what Charleston needed—and fast.

First to voice that sentiment, publicly, was railroad executive John H. Averill, who wrote a letter to the editor of Charleston's *News and Courier* that appeared in October 1899. He made the point that South Carolina was missing out on its fair share of the current international trade boom. What the port city of Charleston lacked specifically, he said, was an instinct for self-promotion. He called for a bold declarative statement directed to the business community at large, saying the city was (still) here, open for business, and receptive to investors from "away." He suggested the staging of a grand exposition to reawaken South Carolina's dormant commercial energy.

Averill's idea found two enthusiastic supporters in *News and Courier* editor J. C. Hemphill and F. W. Wagener, a successful grocery wholesaler who had emigrated to Charleston from Germany. By early 1900 a company had been formed to raise the funds required for making this dream a reality. The exposition was conceived as a celebration to promote the proximity of South Carolina to Latin America in hopes of fostering future trade to ports in Cuba, Haiti, Panama, and Puerto Rico. The organizers dubbed it "The South Carolina Interstate and West Indian Exposition."

Stock subscriptions were sold, and bonds were issued to attract local investors. The company even convinced the state's General Assembly in Columbia to chip in $50,000 as a gesture of good faith. But the enthusiasm shown for the project from the business community was not matched by Charleston's Old Guard aristocracy. They perceived this breast-beating self-promotion as unseemly behavior and largely avoided lending the exposition their financial support. Another blow came when—despite intensive lobbying by Wagener and other investors—the federal government in Washington refused to provide any money to help mount the show. At this time federal funding for expositions like this was usually granted, even generally assumed, but some people said that South Carolina and Charleston still bore the stigma of being the birthplace of secession. And clearly, vivid memories of the Civil War still haunted many Americans at the end of the nineteenth century.

Nevertheless, an ambitious advertising campaign was launched to whip up public interest. The exposition's announced opening was optimistically scheduled for December 1, 1901, and despite the fact that initial funding for the project was disappointing, plans for the exposition pushed ahead.

A site was chosen: 250 acres of land (not surprisingly owned by Wagener) northeast of Charleston along the Ashley River. A principal architect for the project was hired from New York. He was Bradford L. Gilbert, formerly the lead designer of the 1895 Atlanta Exposition. In less than a year, he and a small army of builders and craftsmen transformed the riverside tract of marsh, farm fields, and woods into an idealized metropolis.

Gilbert's architectural vision was manifested in an ornate Spanish Renaissance style, where almost everything was painted a creamy, off-white color. Thus, the exposition was justifiably dubbed "The Ivory City"—a far more memorable label than the fair's tongue-twisting official name.

So rushed was the exposition's assembly that when it officially opened on December 1, 1901, many of the exhibits and some of its buildings were still incomplete. In addition, the heavily advertised opening date turned out to fall on a Sunday, when most of the "Holy City" was quiet and at worshipful rest. Hastily, the noisy hoopla and celebration scheduled for a formal opening had to be rescheduled for the following day. But open, it finally did. And for the next six months, the South Carolina Interstate and West Indian Exposition offered fair-goers an impressive wonderland by day and an electrified fantasy by night. Certainly, most Charlestonians had never seen anything like it.

Gilbert's concept was to divide the 250-acre site into two

major areas: one celebrating Nature and the other an extravaganza of Art. There were themed buildings assigned to both
areas, some sponsored by states or foreign countries and some
representing various industries or cultural topics. In all, twenty
different states chose to participate, none so dramatically as
Pennsylvania, whose building proudly displayed America's historic Liberty Bell. This attracted a good bit of attention among
the mostly Southern visitors who had never been as far North
as Philadelphia.

At a time when racial attitudes in the South were not generally inclusive, there was even a building devoted to African
Americans. The "Negro Department" was headquartered in its
own building and headed by forty-five-year-old Booker T.
Washington.

Most impressive of the structures was the 320-foot-long
Cotton Palace, with its grand colonnade and 75-foot-tall dome.
It was the central focal point of a mall, faced by three major
exhibit halls. The Cotton Palace was flanked by the Palace of
Commerce and the Palace of Agriculture, all facing sunken formal gardens, arched over by bridges for strolling pedestrians.
In these "palaces" were exhibits of the latest industrial ideas
and progressive agricultural techniques, proudly illustrating the
enlightened attitude of South Carolinians.

Dazzling as these displays were, many visitors were far
more attracted to the Midway, a carnival-like section with thrill
rides and rare, exotic amusements. The Midway had also been
a major draw for the Chicago expo. Charleston's version included a House of Horrors, an Eskimo village complete with live
"Eskimos" wearing fur parkas, and a 400-foot long heroic paint-
ing of the Battle of Manassas, with life-sized wax figures of
Robert E. Lee, J. E. B. Stuart, and Stonewall Jackson.

Gentlemen were attracted to the aromatic Turkish Parlor,
where they could smoke imported cigars while live camels, tied
up outside, chewed and spat. Included in the original land-
holdings was Wagener's eighteenth-century plantation house,

Lowndes Grove, which was used as the exposition's Women's Building. Here, crafts and handiwork deemed of interest to the ladies were displayed.

The man-made, forty-acre Lake Juanita contained a fleet of Venetian gondolas for hire. Trained gondoliers could push the sleek boats through the shallow waters and carry visitors through this temporary architectural fantasy—for a price. At the hub of several walkways stood an ornate bandstand, in which musical concerts were performed daily to the delight of passersby.

At night the entire Court of Palaces was ablaze with lights—a heart-stopping display of electric wizardry for many fair-goers who had never seen it used on such a scale before.

Unfortunately, one key ingredient was missing from this heady mix planned by the exposition's founders and investors: a steady stream of ticket-buying people. Perhaps the organizers underestimated the amount of disposable income regional Southerners were willing to spend on such a diversion. Maybe the expo came too soon after Atlanta's similar effort, or perhaps it lacked the global appeal of the successful St. Louis fair, yet to open.

At first the numbers looked good. The average daily attendance of 3,700 people was more than the organizers expected. But many of those who entered the gates did so with heavily discounted tickets, or they came in as "official" guests of one event or another. On its best day ever, May 22, 1902, the exposition attracted slightly more than 25,000 people. In all, the total gate count for Charleston's six-month run was a dismal 675,000—a far cry from the 27 million visitors who had flocked to Chicago's fair by 1894. The numbers just didn't add up to a profit.

Toward the end of the run, a few dignitaries and celebrities showed up but this really didn't change the final outcome. Even Congress voted to send a little money to try and stabilize the expo's crumbling financial foundation, but by then the backers were already in the process of filing for bankruptcy.

President "Teddy" Roosevelt had been scheduled to make an appearance in February 1902, but he was distracted and didn't manage to arrive in Charleston until April, a month before the exposition closed. One of the early motion-picture cameras from Thomas Edison's "invention factory" was on hand to record a fleeting image of the president and his entourage touring the Court of Palaces. His attendance at the exposition prompted what the Edison promoters hyped as "one of the greatest crowds of people ever seen in a motion picture." But that same month, when the famously frank Samuel Clemens, known the world over as Mark Twain, toured the grounds, he wrote back to his wife, "Nobody was there."

In another echo of the Chicago fair, Charleston's exposition made such a stunning first impression that the visitor hardly noticed the palaces and statuary were temporary, lightweight stage settings. Built to last only six months, most of the exhibit halls were little more than ornate sheds of wood and iron scaffolding, plastered over with a thin coat of sawdust, stucco, and paint.

When the money ran out, the magic vanished very quickly. The dismantling of The Ivory City started early in 1902, before the summer heat and humidity settled in over Charleston. Before long almost nothing remained of the once-grand exposition save for the memories and dashed hopes of its backers. Within two years most of the buildings were gone.

The land was soon developed in various other ways. The largest area of what had been the expo's site was taken over by The Citadel when the famous military college moved from its crowded quarters in downtown Charleston to the spacious riverside location. The college built a campus around what had been the expo's parade grounds.

The city bought the area once known as the Court of Palaces and created an urban park. It was named for Confederate hero and former South Carolina Governor Wade

Hampton, who had visited the fair shortly before his death. Although reconfigured and heavily remodeled, two original features of the 1901 exposition have actually managed to survive in Hampton Park. The bandstand has been moved several times and changed in major ways, but its bones are authentic, at least. And the sunken garden of the Court of Palaces has been transformed into a reflecting pond, inhabited by tame ducks kept fat and happy by the children visiting the park. Occasionally, flocks of Canada geese pause in the waters as they fly over Charleston in their yearly migration.

The bandstand and reflecting pond share an odd legacy. They are almost the only traces that remain of a little-known but huge struggle that took place in the South thirty-five years or so *after* the guns of the Civil War fell silent. As the state tried to economically reawaken from the long night that followed the war, there was the interrupting razzle and dazzle of the South Carolina Interstate and West Indian Exhibition of 1901. It rang and flashed and briefly made a little noise until 1902. But the state (and especially the port of Charleston) just rolled over, hit the snooze button, and economically fell back asleep. It wasn't until the huge naval guns of World War I sounded a more serious wake-up call that South Carolina's economy finally saw a new day.

Mr. Anderson Takes on Detroit

·1916·

It was a cold night in January, but everybody in and around the sleepy Southern town of Rock Hill was looking forward to the gala celebration planned at the Carolina Hotel downtown. For several days the worrisome war news from Europe had been nearly crowded off the front page by news of the opening. Local talk on the street had been of little else. Weeks ago, more than a thousand invitations were sent out, and among those expected to show up at the door was South Carolina Governor Richard I. Manning. Also on the list of dignitaries was W. W. Ball, editor of *The State*, Columbia, South Carolina's major newspaper. For glamour (and additional publicity on a national scale), James J. Parian, was expected, too. As a top executive at the Curtis Publishing Company, he might give the event media coverage in the *Saturday Evening Post,* delivered to millions of American homes every week.

A few jaunty-looking motor cars cued up outside the hotel door as distinguished guests began to arrive. Inside, the orchestra struck up a bouncy ragtime tune. A host of pretty, young high-school girls, dressed in ruffled party frocks served refreshments as the last of the guests entered the ballroom. Suddenly, a curtain opened and the guest of honor was revealed—radiant—bathed in a brilliant display of electric lights.

All this excitement was focused on the official

introduction of John Gary Anderson's shiny new brainchild, the Anderson automobile. This was no ordinary motorcar brought down from Detroit or any of the other cities currently manufacturing automobiles for the American market. This new Anderson motorcar was actually built in Rock Hill, South Carolina—the product of local ingenuity, uncompromising standards for quality, and stubborn Southern pride.

John Gary Anderson was an entrepreneur in the great American tradition. He was born in 1861 in Lawsonville, North Carolina, where his early life was marked with sadness. Both parents died before John was nine years old, and a grandfather who stepped in to raise the orphaned boy died only six years later. Like many other children faced with more than their share of sorrow, John Gary Anderson seemed to use this hard luck as a catalyst for achievement. He became an extrovert, filled with self-confidence and the assurance that diligence, hard work, and enterprise would surely lead to great things.

He worked as a restaurant manager, a heavy equipment operator, a tenant farmer, and a print shop pressman, and he'd even sold dry goods in a retail store. He saved his money and kept a sharp eye on any opportunity to make a smart investment.

In 1888, two years after he married Alice Holler, the daughter of a Rock Hill furniture retailer, he opened a small bicycle-repair shop behind his father-in-law's store. For extra income he used his spare time to build horse-drawn buggies. The population of Rock Hill was growing, as was all of York County after the Civil War. Anderson's sturdy, well-built buggies were in great demand; in fact, the newly formed Rock Hill Buggy Company quickly evolved and pushed the bicycle-repair business aside. By 1898 the company had moved into a 45,000-square-foot manufacturing plant.

Anderson constantly toyed with his product, making small improvements that were attractive to customers. He invented and patented an axle that outlasted any of his competitors'.

Best of all, it could be oiled right on the buggy without having to remove the wheels.

Early on, he understood the power of advertising and spent thousands of dollars on newspaper ads, billboards, and signs. By 1911 the Rock Hill Buggy Company was one of the South's leading buggy manufacturers, with total sales of more than 80,000 carriages and a net worth of $6 million. An article published in the *Atlanta Journal* that same year hailed Anderson's product as "the best buggy ever built for the price . . . [and] that the South could compete with Yankee Doodle in genius . . . thrift and economy."

Even as his buggy business was flourishing, the now-wealthy Rock Hill industrialist was contemplating a foray into the emerging automotive market. In 1910 he announced plans to build an automobile. He said it would seat four, feature a 30-horsepower, 4-cylinder engine, and "sell for $1,600—complete with magneto, batteries, gas lights, generator, oil side lamps, tail light, horn, coat rail, detachable rims, tire tools, compound pump, jack, and tool kit." This ambitious early promise never actually materialized, but it testifies to Anderson's enthusiasm for the idea.

By 1914 an important tide had turned in America. Sales of horse-drawn buggies had dropped by a third. People were interested in automobiles. What had started out as something of a fad was fast becoming a viable American industry. Soon, Anderson's buggy business was in serious trouble. In response—almost as an offering to appease the competitive giant threatening his business (namely, Henry Ford)—Anderson announced a new line: a series of auto bodies especially built to fit onto the chassis of the phenomenally popular Model T. Meanwhile, he continued dreaming about and planning his own automobile.

"We had to do something," he recalled in the lengthy autobiography he penned later in life. "We had a big factory full of machinery, and it could not be allowed to stand still. The

Automobile—while new in many respects," he continued, "was a kindred line, and our equipment was suitable to handling it on a small scale."

Six cars were built as prototypes in 1915. When they were tested and proved ready, the Anderson automobile made its formal debut in 1916 at the biggest party Rock Hill had seen in years. It was called the "6-40-6," and it was splendid, in a quality-over-style kind of way. It rode on twelve-spoke wheels, and had Westinghouse electrical equipment (including a trouble lamp and a cigar lighter) plus a six-cylinder engine that offered the power of thirty-eight horses at 200 rpm. The speedometer went up to a dazzling 60 mph. There were two basic body styles: a three-passenger roadster and a four-passenger touring car. Unless otherwise specified by the buyer, it came in a smart Brewster green, with black fenders and a black hood.

The Detroit-based automotive press gave the Anderson automobile fair odds for success, saying, "It would appeal to Southerners since they could save up to $50 in freight charges" over cars manufactured in the North. Whether or not this was the main incentive, the Anderson Motor Company had orders for an estimated 1,200 cars by 1917, which translated into $1 million in sales. That same year the company had a payroll of $100,000.

Even as the country's entry into World War I curtailed auto sales around the nation, Anderson won a lucrative government contract to manufacture small army trucks and trailers. His future couldn't have looked brighter. The car's best year was 1920, when a total of 1,280 units rolled out of the factory. By that time there was a convertible three-seater, a five-passenger touring model, and a big, six-passenger convertible that sold for $1,675. The top-of-the-line sedan went for a whopping $2,550. There were 150 dealers and a commission house in New York City, which handled all international sales.

In a defiant tweak of his nemesis competitor, Henry Ford, Anderson bragged of selling more of his cars in Detroit (right under Mr. Ford's nose) than were sold in all of South Carolina, where the majority of Anderson's stockholders lived! This was indeed a cheeky remark. Ford was relentlessly churning out reliable automobiles for legions of working-class Americans and selling them for between $345 and $760 a pop. Anderson even adopted an advertising slogan that smugly justified the cost difference, "A Little Bit Higher in Price, but—made in *Dixie*."

Another difference between the Anderson and a Ford was its manufacturing process. Every Anderson automobile was essentially assembled (hand-built) from elements manufactured by someone else, somewhere else, who was making a profit on those parts. Ford, on the other hand, started his manufacturing process with raw materials. The rubber for the tires on every new Ford, for instance, came from Ford's own rubber plantations in the tropics and was shipped to Detroit for processing in the holds of Ford-owned ships.

After 1920 the country experienced labor problems exacerbated by the postwar downturn in the national economy. This meant that the first great automotive buying boom was finally over. As never before, price started to be the major factor in most car buyers' minds. Anderson reacted to this by railing against car buyers for not supporting his Southern-based enterprise. He failed to see the handwriting plainly on the wall—his cars cost too much.

Even though the company announced a "new" less expensive model for 1922, financial problems continued to dog Anderson. Ford offered his touring car for $298, whereas Anderson's so-called "cheaper" model sold for $1,195. When Ford instituted an innovative payment option whereby buyers could purchase their cars on a weekly installment plan, the game was over.

In 1924 only 616 Andersons were sold. The following year the Rock Hill auto manufacturer was forced to sell off assets held by the old buggy company, and by 1926 the Anderson

Motor Company couldn't pay its taxes. The enterprise folded after only ten years, having produced 6,300 automobiles for the American market.

John Gary Anderson's ride with Detroit's big boys was spectacular but all too brief. He never fully acknowledged his role in the company's demise: his failure to adapt assembly-line economics or adjust his standards of luxury despite major changes in market demand. He always prided himself on his use of the finest materials and his insistence on the best workmanship. To his credit he was an innovator who gave the American automobile buyer a number of firsts: He pioneered construction of the first motorized convertible top and the foot-operated light dimmer, and he offered a rainbow of colors when everyone else was using black, gray, or green.

Anderson spent the final decade of his life in retirement, living at the large family home in Rock Hill or visiting their Florida retreat. He wrote a rambling, 900-page autobiography, in which he mostly defended his business decisions and recounted his many accomplishments.

Of the nearly 6,300 Andersons built during the company's operation, only a handful are known to still exist. One is on display in the South Carolina State Museum in Columbia, another is in the Antique Automobile Museum in Myrtle Beach, and yet another is in Rock Hill. To most car buffs the Anderson is a short footnote to America's love affair with the automobile—a love story mostly played out among the industrial smokestacks of Detroit. But on that cold rainy night in Rock Hill in 1916, the Anderson was the toast of Dixie.

Porgy: The Myth and the Man

·1924·

Samuel "Goat" Smalls was born in 1889 on James Island, South Carolina, one of twenty children born to Elvira Smalls in a small clapboard cabin, originally built for slaves, somewhere across the Ashley River from Charleston. He lived out his brief life story in the damp streets and crumbling tenements of Charleston in the years before and shortly after World War I.

Early in Sammy's childhood—when he was about five or six years old—his legs were paralyzed, probably by a bout with spinal meningitis. From that age forward he never walked again; he got around by dragging himself along with his arms. As he reached maturity, those arms would grow powerful from their unusual burden. Indeed, they were stronger than most workingmen's arms. When Sammy needed to travel greater distances, he used an improvised homemade cart mounted on four wheels, which he hitched to a goat. Reins attached to the goat's horns allowed Sammy to steer his cart fairly well from place to place.

In the 1950s, when his mother was near the end of her life, Elvira Smalls was quoted as saying Sammy "crossed the river" into Charleston as a teenager and she "lost track of him" after that. For some families during those years, the world could be very small.

In Charleston Sammy and his goat cart were soon a

regular sight around the busy wharves that stretched along the Cooper River. Everybody in Charleston was poor, it seemed. But those who spent their days working and sweating along the waterfront had it especially bad. Sammy was usually seen in the company of fishermen from the Mosquito Fleet, a group of small fishing boats that went out into Charleston Harbor at dawn each morning to bring back the fresh seafood typically served on Charlestonian dinner tables later in the day.

Sammy was popular with these fishermen because his powerful arm muscles enabled him to haul in the heaviest nets, gorged with fish and shrimp headed for market. He was a good oarsman, too, able to keep a rudder steady when the tide or the weather suddenly turned. These black fishermen gave Sammy his nickname, "Porgy," after the small fish known by that name caught in the shallows off the nearby barrier islands.

Sammy's powerful torso also caught the eye of many women, by all accounts. Despite his useless legs he was known to be quite the ladies' man along the waterfront. They called him a "road sport"; in other words, he "got around." He mixed it up with the rough-and-tumble sailors who worked along the Cooper River wharves, as well, and was frequently listed in the local newspaper's "police blotter" as being arrested for street fights and rowdiness. Locals recall how he always carried a switchblade or a straight razor in his goat cart.

Once he was actually charged with murder, in some kind of disagreement over the affections of a woman. He was held in the old jail on Charleston's Magazine Street until a group of benevolent Charleston businessmen argued with authorities to release him on a plea of self-defense. Sammy Smalls had earned some measure of respect from these men, possibly because he never saw himself as an invalid. He always managed to support himself (and apparently several women, too) without charity or complaint. He took care of his own, and that earned him favors—more than once—with influential white men in the city.

Old-time fishermen used to say he loved to go with them to Remley's Point, off Mount Pleasant, where the men and their families would combine a festive beach picnic with the job of scraping barnacles off their boats. The end result was often a boozy weekend of work, good food, and some seaside romance for the young folks.

For most of his life, Sammy's address is a mystery. Some say he lived "uptown" in a run-down section of old wooden houses then known as Coolblow Village because of the sea breeze that sometimes blew in from the southeast during the sweltering summertime. Others say he lived near Charleston's infamous red-light district. No one can say for sure.

It is known that Sammy's last years were spent living in Cabbage Row, a crowded tenement on Church Street, where black families found shelter in property that had stood abandoned since the days of Reconstruction. And during this time they say he took a common-law wife. Downtown residents remember him selling "grungers," small sweet cakes, from a stand at the corner of King and George Streets. If he wasn't there, he and his goat cart could usually be found right out on Broad Street, at a stand set up outside the law office of one of his influential white "friends."

Even Charleston's indomitable flower ladies succumbed to Porgy's charm. They would feed his goat the wilted blossoms left over from any not-too-profitable selling day. Sammy was a Charleston institution, taken for granted just like the city's charming old town houses draped in wisteria every spring.

Then one day somebody remarked, "Say, I haven't seen Sammy around lately. Have you?"

"No," came the answer. "Can't say that I have."

Not long afterward, Sammy's "wife" was seen driving the familiar goat cart back across the Ashley River Bridge toward James Island. The frail figure in the back of the cart was Sammy, ravaged by venereal disease and by the excesses of a life lived too fast. He was going back to the cabin of his birth.

Although he was only thirty-five, life had nearly consumed him. There he would die and go to an unmarked grave. Only months later, reborn as the character Porgy in Dubose Heyward's famous novel, he would become world famous in literature and (eventually) in the annals of American song.

When Charleston writer Dubose Heyward (1885–1940) wrote *Porgy*, it was the first major Southern novel to portray blacks in roles that weren't submissive to whites. He was breaking new literary ground. His fictionalized main character, Porgy, was so complicated and multidimensional that critics still argue about whether this man was a romantic hero or a tragic, naive buffoon. Heyward, too, grew up on Church Street, not far away from Cabbage Row, then an enclave of poor black families. In the novel it's called "Catfish Row." Here, black vendors set up vegetable stands along the street to hawk their produce to shoppers walking by. In the 1920s that section of Church Street was suffering hard times. Many of the old pre-Revolutionary homes had been sold for taxes and had fallen into disrepair. Poor blacks crowded into the low-rent slums eking out a living any way they could. No doubt Heyward drew on these early childhood memories as he created Porgy's world for his famous novel.

Other tantalizing glimpses of Sammy Smalls's life occasionally peek through the lines of Heyward's story. In Heyward's novel the principal characters all depart the heat and humidity of Catfish Row for a weekend outing on the fictional island of Kittiwake. Such boat parties to sea-island getaways were quite common in Sammy's day. Small, steam-powered paddle wheelers could be chartered for day trips and excursions to the mostly uninhabited barrier islands off Charleston for a pleasant summertime diversion. The women would pack food enough to supplement what fish and crab they'd catch for eating, and the men would bring along enough moonshine liquor to make surefire trouble before the weekend ran out. Kittiwake was Heyward's substitute name for Kiawah, now a world-famous luxury island resort.

No one knows if Sammy ever made it over to Kiawah for one of those 1920s outings. But the obvious similarities between Sammy "Goat" Smalls and the character Porgy are intriguing. Other details from Heyward's novel are hard to pin down as being directly related to Sammy's life. Clearly, Heyward used artistic license liberally in his famous work of fiction. Any real illumination of Sammy Smalls's life story blinks and sputters like a lamp low on oil. Long periods pass with little or nothing known of his whereabouts or general welfare. Still, there *was* a crippled black vendor named Porgy; that much is true. Did he endure a tragic love for a drug-addicted woman named Bess? Did she leave him for the bright lights and pleasure domes of New York? The lines between fact and urban legend have long ago blurred.

The early death of Sammy Smalls might have been foreseen as a predictable outcome, given his circumstances and the limits of his resources. But Porgy, the literary figure, lived on to fame and fortune.

Heyward's novel was published in 1925. He collaborated with his wife, Dorothy, on a version for the New York stage a year later. It delighted audiences and confused critics, who were forced to rethink long-established racial stereotypes. A decade after the play was a hit on Broadway, the story (once more a la Heyward) was immortalized in a work, now accepted as a masterpiece, by famous composer George Gershwin. This work, *Porgy and Bess,* introduced a new musical idiom— the American folk opera. New York's Theatre Guild produced the opera version. Although it was never a staggering financial success (very little was in the Depression year of 1935), the music was eventually hailed as a great work of art. Porgy, the fictional character, was a manufactured persona who so completely outgrew the person who inspired him that the life and times of the real man have been lost. In fact, many of the literary academics and sophisticates from the world of opera have no idea that a "real" Porgy ever existed.

In a quiet graveyard on James Island in South Carolina, Sammy Smalls was all but forgotten, but in 1987, sixty-three years after his death, a self-appointed committee of Charleston businessmen, recalling Sammy and his goat cart, finally erected a monument over the man's unmarked grave. It reads: SAMMY "GOAT" SMALLS . . . THE INSPIRATION FOR DUBOSE HEYWARD'S NOVEL *PORGY*, AND LATER THE OPERA *PORGY AND BESS* BY HEYWARD AND GERSH-WIN. Credit finally was given where ultimately credit was due.

Brookgreen Gardens: Oasis of Art and Nature

· 1930 ·

Archer Milton Huntington was immediately captivated by the photographs of the ancient, moss-draped live oaks whose huge boughs reached high and low, spreading a welcoming, if ethereal, canopy of shade. The South Carolina Lowcountry landscape seemed to reach out and beckon him with its timeless beauty and serenity. The real estate brochure had landed on his desk quite accidentally, but he found himself pouring over every word and picture of this magical place. It seemed a long way from the hustle and bustle of New York life and the pressures of the railroad and shipping businesses. And the timing could not have been better, because the doctor had just advised a warmer climate to improve his beloved wife's failing health. The couple would plan a trip at once to visit the area and investigate the intriguing options.

Huntington and his wife, Anna Hyatt Huntington, set out on their yacht in 1929 to travel down the Intracoastal Waterway and were struck by the beguiling scenery that greeted them along the way, especially in the Waccamaw River region. They were unprepared for what they saw at every turn—the sweeping marsh vistas, the ubiquitous creeks and inlets, the mysterious swamplands, the sandy pine forests, and those majestic oak trees. The overwhelming natural beauty and its abundant wildlife had transported them into another world altogether.

The couple was receptive to the call of the Carolina Lowcountry perhaps more than some because of their artistic interests and pursuits. Industrialist Archer Huntington was heir to the transportation fortunes of his stepfather, Collis P. Huntington, but he was also a sensitive philanthropist, historian, and poet. Anna Hyatt Huntington was a renowned sculptor seeking a venue for her growing body of work. In early 1930 they purchased four adjoining, former rice and indigo plantations in South Carolina called The Oaks, Brookgreen, Springfield, and Laurel Hill between the towns of Murrell's Inlet and Pawleys Island, just south of Myrtle Beach. Together the properties covered more than 9,000 acres and were a part of the original land grants to brothers John and William Allston from King George II of England in the early 1720s.

The property's history reflects the story of the rice culture of the South Carolina coast. The cultivation of rice thrived with the importation of slaves from West Africa. These slaves brought with them a knowledge of the intricacies associated with raising this profitable crop. The land, with its tidal creeks and freshwater estuaries, and the climate, with its long growing season, offered an ideal locale. The cheap labor provided an almost inexhaustible supply of strong backs to clear swampland, build dikes, and transform the natural landscape into a wealth-building enterprise.

With the end of slavery after the Civil War, the rice culture began a decline from which it was never able to recover. Depressed economic conditions in the South and the loss of the labor supply forced planters into the sharecropping system. Former slaves who remained on the plantations grew their own crops, "paying" their rent by giving a share of each harvest to the landowner. Toward the end of the nineteenth and beginning of the twentieth centuries, a series of devastating storms and hurricanes wreaked havoc on the expansive rice fields. The once-prosperous rice culture capitulated to economic decline as well as the forces of nature. Nature began its gradual process of reclaiming her lands as swamp and forest.

None of this history was lost on the new owners/stewards of this site. The Huntingtons began designing a winter home and garden setting for Anna's sculpture that was respectful of the land's past while enhancing the splendid natural environment. They recognized immediately that the setting would make an ideal wildlife sanctuary as well. Construction of their winter home began in 1931 and continued for three years intermittently between work on the garden. Mr. Huntington insisted that local labor be employed for the construction, wishing to create work for area residents struggling during the Great Depression. They called the home *Atalaya,* the Spanish word for "watchtower." Archer Huntington was a noted scholar of Spanish history and indulged his passion by designing the house in the Moorish style of architecture found along the Mediterranean coast.

The one-story building was laid out in a square shape, with a central, open courtyard. The front wall faced the beach and the Atlantic Ocean, and it contained, along with its two adjoining perimeter walls, thirty rooms that made up the living areas. These consisted of a number of bedrooms and baths, a dining room, kitchen, sunroom, library, and servants' quarters. Mr. Huntington's study, his secretary's office, and Mrs. Huntington's indoor and outdoor studios made up the southern wing. Because Anna Huntington often sculpted animals in her work, horse stables, dog kennels, and even a bear pen were part of the facilities. At Atalaya the 40-foot tall, central "watchtower" served a very utilitarian purpose other than its architectural legacy. It contained a 3,000-gallon, cypress-lined water tank that created the necessary water pressure for running water throughout the house. The Huntingtons' new winter residence paid homage to South Carolina with the landscaping of the inner courtyard. There Archer Huntington specified the abundant planting of the Sabal palmetto (or common name "cabbage" palmetto), the state tree of South Carolina.

The garden they set out to create at Brookgreen Plantation was to be unlike any other. Archer Huntington envisioned the space as a tribute to his wife's art and a testament of his love for her. Anna took her inspiration from him and sketched out the design of the garden walkways in the shape of a butterfly with outstretched wings. She incorporated into the central space the original homesite and magnificent allée of oaks from its early plantation days. Six large millstones that had been used for hulling rice were placed about a terrace. A serpentine, open brickwork wall was built to define the grounds without closing in the spectacular landscape. Mr. Huntington saw that plaques, engraved with the verses of great poets, adorned niches in the walls, complementing the inspirational and meditative quality of the garden's experience.

They soon realized that the treasure they had discovered for themselves was beginning to take on a larger life. In 1931 they set up a private, nonprofit organization with the goal of showcasing American figurative sculpture set within an outdoor surrounding of native plants and animals. Anna Huntington invited other sculptors to place their work there, and it soon became renowned as the place to view some of the best sculpture of the nineteenth and twentieth centuries. The following year the gardens were opened to the public, and Brookgreen became the first sculpture garden in the United States.

The Huntingtons enjoyed their oasis of tranquility for many years, refining and adding to the garden and its sculpture collection. Archer Huntington described Brookgreen Gardens as

a quiet joining of hands between science and art . . .
[that] has gradually found extension in an outline col-

lection representative of the history of American sculpture, from the 19th century, which find its natural setting out of doors. . . . Its object is the presentation of the natural life of a given district as a museum . . . it is a garden, and gardens have from early times been rightly embellished by the art of the sculptor, that principle has found expression in American creative art.

After Mr. Huntington's death in 1955, Atalaya's furnishings were sent to the Huntingtons' New York home, and Mrs. Huntington's studio equipment was transferred to Brookgreen Gardens' new studio. In 1960 Atalaya and the surrounding acreage was leased to the state of South Carolina by the Brookgreen trustees. Mrs. Huntington died in 1973, leaving behind the legacy of the couple's creative vision and thoughtful realization of a dream.

At present the unfurnished house and its 3-mile oceanfront site make up Huntington Beach State Park on U.S. Highway 17 South. Directly across the highway Brookgreen Gardens displays more than 550 works of American sculpture selected from more than 700 pieces in its permanent collection. Beginning with the stunning, monolithic *Fighting Stallions* by Anna Hyatt Huntington at the Gardens' entrance, other noted works include sculpture by Lena Goodacre, Gertrude Vanderbilt Whitney, Augustus Saint-Gaudens, Paul Manship, Gutzon Borglum, and Daniel Chester French. What the Huntingtons started by pulling together the talents and energies of so many gifted artisans became something greater than the sum of its parts. Indeed, Brookgreen Gardens became an eden of beauty, an oasis of art and nature, a treasure for South Carolina, and an invaluable gift to the American people.

Brookgreen Gardens is on the National Register of Historic Places and is designated a National Historic Landmark.

It is one of only twelve institutions in the United States accredited by the American Association of Museums as well as the American Zoo and Aquarium Association. The gardens contain 2,000 species and subspecies of native plants plus a fifty-acre aviary and wildlife park of native animals.

Charleston Adopts a Preservation Ethic
· 1931 ·

Over and over, tourists in Charleston hear the cliche, "After the Civil War, Charlestonians were too poor to paint but too proud to whitewash. So they did nothing. That's how the old buildings survived." The problem with cliches is that they're often based on half-truths or meaningless generalities. And on the way toward glib abbreviation, the truth gets sadly cheated every time.

Charleston's famous preservation ethic has never been the result of mere economic duress, nor has it resulted from stagnant Southern pride. Instead, it's been the product of hard work and the personal sacrifice of a few early visionaries. Once the foundations were laid, however, the preservation movement grew, and it has been supported ever since by the discipline of constant political pressure. That fact makes it quite a story.

Many people assume that the uncanny preservation of Charleston's early architecture began in 1920 with the formation of the Society for the Preservation of Old Dwellings (forerunner of the present-day Preservation Society of Charleston), spearheaded by the remarkable Susan Pringle Frost. That was clearly a key milestone, but the city's preservation impulse actually awakened much earlier.

Evidence of a reverence for the city's colonial past and the city's architectural legacy appeared as early as 1835. The congregation of St. Philip's Episcopal Church was faced with the dilemma of rebuilding the original structure (destroyed by fire) or replacing it with something new and more modern. Discussing the issue in comparative terms, a church member wrote at the time:

> Let the old large private dwellings in Charleston be compared with those more recently built, and I am very much mistaken, if the general, as well as the scientific, and the tasteful eye will not give the former the reference. The comparison holds good in favour of the old public buildings also, and more particularly of the Churches . . . York-minster was so re-built as to be scarcely distinguishable from its predecessor, and why not St. Philip's?

Another marker surfaced in 1853 when a South Carolinian, Ann Pamela Cunningham, started a movement to rescuc from developers in Virginia the badly neglected plantation home of President George Washington. She made an appeal for funds to support her newly formed Mount Vernon Ladies Association in the *Charleston Mercury,* counting on finding a sympathetic audience among the readership of this local newspaper.

The streak of basic conservatism that runs deep through the Charlestonian mindset was described in an 1857 article in *Harper's Weekly.* Their architectural critic said, "There are two Charlestons; the old and the new—representing rival communities. The old," he wrote, "is formidable in sheer stubbornness and . . . very immovable. [They] spend a great deal of money furbishing up the old."

An observer from New York in 1860 said she "admired Charlestonians who lived in quaint old residences—showing their occupants had grandparents."

The words preservation and ethic were possibly combined for the first time by writer Arthur Mazyck in his guidebook to the city published in 1875:

> Beautiful as a dream, tinged with romance, conse-
> crated by tradition, glorified by history, rising from
> the very bosom of the waves, like a fairy city created
> by the enchanter's wand. . . . That was, and is,
> Charleston, thanks to her people's preservation ethic.

The survival of so many historic buildings from Charleston's eighteenth- and nineteenth-century heydays can hardly be an accident. The often-mentioned designation of post–Civil War poverty as the genesis of the movement is illogical, for times of economic duress are far more conducive to the decay and destruction of urban fabric than are periods of relative prosperity. The conscious preservation of a city's architectural heritage is an expensive endeavor, and it demands dedication, discipline, and an underlying resource of human energy.

For Charleston that energy may have been supplemented by the advent of the internal-combustion engine—the automobile. In the years following World War I, Charleston became a regular stop for automobile travelers heading south from New York to Florida. Especially at first, when ownership of automobiles was somewhat restricted to the well-to-do, these travelers stopped frequently to shop and collect "souvenirs" of their travels. They were particularly fascinated by Charleston's cache of colonial ironwork, fine paneling, and other "collectible" architectural resources. This curiosity for the old and quaint, a genuine appreciation for its high quality of craftsmanship, and the economic distress of its owners joined forces and became a legitimate assault on the architectural heritage of the city.

So real was this threat to the very soul of what gives Charleston its identity that the civic reaction was the formation of the Society for the Preservation of Old Dwellings in 1920, led by Susan Pringle Frost, a vigorous and forward-thinking individual. As a suffragette, champion of women's education, real estate agent, and amateur restoration contractor—she took no prisoners. Her energy, dedication, and personal sacrifice have become a Charleston legend. The group's first order of business was to protect the Joseph Manigault House, designed about 1803 by Charleston's famous gentleman architect, Gabriel Manigault. This handsome Adamesque-style masterpiece was scheduled for demolition to be replaced, ironically, by a gasoline station.

The crisis of the Manigault House was only the beginning. Soon came a similar threat to the Heyward-Washington House, built in 1770 and visited by George Washington in 1791. In this case a collector wanted to remove its valuable interior paneling for installation in another house in a distant city.

The heroic effort to save both houses reads like a suspense novel, complete with sacrifice, bravery, and exciting wins and tragic losses on both sides. Suffice it to say, the thirty-two dedicated "zealots for preservation" who followed Miss Frost's lead were fully engaged by the challenge. Their early victories were an important first step. But a decade later, the group found it necessary to reinforce their intentions with some legal backbone. Neither the will of the preservation organization's founders nor the city's longstanding preservation ethic could stand up indefinitely to the forces of easy development and quick profit.

Fortunately for Charleston and its future, the mayor at the time was Thomas Porcher Stoney, a man with deep ties to the city's old plantation society and a champion of the city's storied past. In 1929 he began working toward what would become Charleston's most significant contribution to the preservation movement in America, the nation's first Historic District Zoning Ordinance, adopted in 1931. The ordinance provided for the designation of a defined historic district (originally a small section in the oldest part of Charleston), but it included the important option of being expanded in the future. It also established a Board of Architectural Review, which had governance over demolition and alteration of historic structures. It even had "aesthetic control" over the construction of new buildings within the district.

This breakthrough law took preservation (not just in Charleston but everywhere) to a new level. It moved beyond the saving of one or two important houses at a time to the sweeping legal protection of an entire historic environment.

Through subsequent years the boundaries of Charleston's Old and Historic District have been expanded many times. At present it is the largest historic district of its kind in America. Each time the boundaries are extended, however, the old battle between the preservation ethic versus the trend toward modernization and the chance to make a fast dollar have been rejoined. A new generation of preservationists maintains the vigil and seeks a balance of the ever-changing economic scales. Undoubtedly this is one of the reasons 4.3 million visitors come to see the city each year and enjoy its hospitality. Now Charleston's preservation ethic is world famous, a model for communities everywhere hoping to escape the quicksand of aesthetic (and therefore cultural) homogenization.

Albert Simons, who was for most of the twentieth century Charleston's premier preservation architect, wrote in 1923:

> In our present day quest for progress and modernity, which is altogether to be commended, let us not ignore the value of this great heritage, which is far more valuable than mere pedantry and more vital than mere sentiment; it is nothing less than the record of the ideals of a people.

Headin' South of the Border

· 1933 ·

It was the bottom of the Great Depression: 1933. Alan Schafer was studying journalism at the University of South Carolina in Columbia. Like about everyone else during those years, he was struggling to make ends meet. Still, he was a quick-witted fellow, a fast talker, and a hit with the girls. What he sometimes lacked in enthusiasm for his classes he made up for in personal charm. He also had an uncanny ability to make a fast dollar whenever he really needed one.

One day, a phone call came from home with the news that Alan's father, a small-time cafe owner and local beer distributor, had fallen seriously ill. In short Alan learned that his college days would have to go on hold until better times came along. For now he was needed at home to help keep his father's business going. With sadness young Schafer packed up his belongings and left campus life and his good times there behind forever. He went back to the little cafe his parents ran in upstate South Carolina, where fate and, eventually, a fortune awaited.

Prohibition was on its way out. America was more than ready to imbibe without fear of public arrest or entanglement with organized crime. Alan saw this as an opportunity for profit. He convinced his father to sell the family cafe and concentrate on distributing beer. He opened what he called "The Beer Depot" on the South Carolina side of the state line, just across from North Carolina's Robeson County.

When Prohibition was finally repealed in 1935, Robeson County's commissioners had voted to keep their county piously "dry." Because Schafer's place was literally 10 feet shy of the North Carolina state line, he named it South of the Border Beer Depot. Not surprisingly, the enterprise became very popular with his beer-thirsty neighbors to the north. In fact, Schafer's Beer Depot became something of a political lightning rod. Certain North Carolina teetotalers angrily objected to Schafer's blatant operation, saying it "flew in the face of their moral values."

To appease these people Schafer promised to downplay the beer sales and promote the food and souvenir side of his business. He changed the sign to read SOUTH OF THE BORDER DRIVE-IN. This seemed to satisfy the neighbors to the north, for the time being.

Schafer's modest 18-by-36 foot cinderblock building with steel doors and iron bars on the windows, was anything but grand. There was a three-acre, unpaved parking lot for cars, and inside there was a grill for cooking burgers and a lunch counter with ten secondhand stools. Even though the building was somewhat rough looking, patrons found it appealing enough to keep Schafer's cash register ringing. And, of course, there was the added attraction of beer.

During these years drive-ins were all the rage. The edited sign—minus any reference to beer sales—meant that it appealed to road-weary families as well as thirsty locals. Soon, business was so good that Schafer sometimes had to keep a farm tractor on-site to rescue the customers whose cars became mired to their axles in parking-lot mud.

Meanwhile, as Schafer watched the action surrounding his roadside "Drive-in," he started to notice an interesting trend. After the gas rationing and travel restrictions of World War II were lifted, he saw hoards of restless young families taking to the American roads, specifically streaming down U.S. Highway 301 to coastal vacations in the South. He thought it might be a good idea to offer these travelers a place to stop for a meal and maybe a souvenir or two.

Originally, his "Depot Drive-in" business required only three employees, but by 1954, traffic had improved to the point where Schafer could add twenty motel rooms to his mix of food, souvenirs, (and—shhh—beer). From that point on the constant building boom at South of the Border never ceased.

A Mexican theme evolved from the "Border" part of the name, and that soon took on a life of its own. Schafer started using roadside billboards to attract customers to his establishment. The more signs he rented, the more business he found. Somewhere along the line, he introduced a vaguely Hispanic cartoon character named Pedro to do the talking. Pedro was short, overweight, rather lazy, and always seemed to have an oversized sombrero pulled low over his eyes. The billboards were also painted in gaudy, Day-Glo colors, impossible to miss. Pedro was anything but politically correct, but in the less-sensitive mid-fifties, auto travelers, especially the children, seemed to find him amusing. Eventually, teaser billboards with Pedro advertising South of the Border stretched from Maine to Florida. This billboard barrage continues today.

PEDRO SEZ, NO MONEY BUSINESS, JOOST YANKEE PANKY, reads one, in a mock Mexican accent that sets back Pan-American race relations a good fifty years.

Another reads, LONG TIME NO SI! SI PEDRO TODAY. SIESTA TOMORROW! Here, Pedro is clearly telling drivers to keep driving; good times lay ahead at South of the Border.

As the signs grow more frequent, the message becomes more targeted to the destination and what it has to offer. YOU'RE ALWAYS A WEINER WITH PEDRO suggesting the fast-food options awaiting travelers who stop. Not even the heat of South Carolina's relentless summer sun escapes being used for promotional purposes: WHEN YOU'RE HOT, YOU'RE HOT. COOL EET WEETH PEDRO. Early on, South of the Border offered air conditioning.

Nearer the state line billboards appear about every mile. If the children in the car haven't taken the bait by this time, it's the adults who are now under siege. As the hours of tedious driving through seemingly endless miles of flat, open countryside start to prey on a road-weary mind, another billboard appears with the coup de grace, TOO TIRED TO TANGO? REST WITH PEDRO TONIGHT.

Off in the distance, a first glimpse of the destination appears. A giant, lime-green sombrero looms on the horizon, with its zigzag painted trim. It's actually a 200-foot-tall observation tower, ablaze in lights by night, rising out of Dillon County landscape.

When patrons stop, and they do—sometimes 40,000 of them on any given summer weekend—they discover Pedro isn't just a figment of headlight hypnosis. He's a 97-foot-tall, seventy-seven-ton version of the billboard mascot, holding a giant sign that says in undeniable neon, you're at SOUTH OF THE BORDER. Cars can drive between his massive bowed legs (planted 18 feet deep in the hard South Carolina clay). Just beyond him lies a wonderland of roadside adventures.

The 350-acre attraction features fourteen gift shops, six restaurants, 300 motel rooms, plus the observation tower shaped like a giant sombrero. There's an ice-cream parlor, a fireworks store, three gas stations, and kiddie rides. The Linen Store does a brisk business; so does the Leather Shop. There's a Mexican Shop East, a Mexican Shop West, and a miniature golf course—if shopping isn't every traveler's cup of tequila.

These days, Pedro is getting a bit long in the tooth. He's now on the downside of his fifth decade, but he's still going strong. Schafer never apologized for capitalizing on his little ethnic stereotype. When a Mexican embassy official passing through the state complained that Pedro's image was insulting to Latinos everywhere, Schafer countered, "Look, I've got one hundred employees here working at good-paying jobs—above minimum wage. I could use some more! Why don't you send your Mexicans here to work for me?" Schafer went on to say he never heard another word from the embassy, and shrugged, "They just lost a chance to give one hundred Mexicans good jobs." At one point the payroll for South of the Border included 750 employees.

South of the Border's alchemy seems to defy the slings and arrows of both recession and boom. The crowds who stop at the roadside attraction have changed over time, and they spend money in different ways, for different reasons. But a certain core group always seems to find what they want. The all-time, best-selling souvenir is a small glass ashtray (made in Taiwan) that bears Pedro's likeness and a South of the Border logo. It sells for 50 cents. There's a South of the Border baseball cap for $7.95, and a Pedro Placemat goes for a dollar and a half. True connoisseurs like to take home a 3-foot-long flyswatter labeled "Pedro's Bug Buster; $3.50."

In 1999 Pedro went "Hollywood." South of the Border was featured in Stephen Spielberg's romantic comedy, *Forces of Nature*, starring Ben Affleck and Sandra Bullock. Even *they* made the stop along I–95 on their way to laughter and romance.

Clearly, South of the Border is a marketing phenomenon. Schafer, who died in 2001, was a merchandising genius. He had his faults, like any man, and his political entanglements later in life led him astray of the law. But the facts remain; he made a vast fortune out in the middle of nowhere on what had been scrubby corn and tobacco fields. He coaxed South Carolinians and millions of transient visitors into spending hard-earned money for anything vaguely Mexican—maracas, sombreros, and even stuffed toy bulls. He convinced countless numbers of hot, tired tourists to detour from their intended destinations, suspend their disbelief, and imagine that this might truly be a Hispanic wonderland at the edge of South Carolina.

Before Disneyland, before Busch Gardens, before the slightly closer Carowinds amusement park appeared just outside Charlotte, North Carolina, there was South of the Border. As Pedro put it, YOU NEVER SAUSAGE A PLACE!

Nazi POWs in Our Own Back Yard

· 1944 ·

It was a pitch-black night in February 1945, and the three German POWs had been incarcerated in the South Carolina Prisoner of War camp for months. The drudgery and monotony of life there had made Privates Max Lauer, Willi Steuer, and Edward Gielen desperate for a way out, and they each crawled under the barbed wire surrounding the compound and hiked their way to the Ten Mile Army Air Base nearby.

Once there, they stole a jeep, disposed of their khaki prison fatigues with the large letters P.W. painted on the back, and donned their full German uniforms complete with combat ribbons, for the trip south down U.S. Highway 17. If caught in civilian attire, they could be accused of spying, a capital offense. On the other hand their prison fatigues labeled them instantly as prisoners of war. Their uniforms seemed the best option, so they naively (or perhaps brazenly) thought traveling in uniform in an American jeep might attract less notice.

The plan was to drive to Savannah, Georgia, a little more than 100 miles away, and stow away on a neutral ship, eventually returning to their homeland. Their belief that Savannah was a neutral port, however was mistaken. (The only two neutral ports in the United States were New York and Philadelphia.) They had also underestimated the keen eyes of the natives of the Lowcountry, because a woman spotted them as they passed through Beaufort. She reported the strange sighting to the authorities, and the fugitives were picked up within the hour.

Almost every state had at least one POW camp during World War II, but the South and the Southwest areas of the country became the most popular sites, due to the mild climate and fewer vital industries located there. Fear of escapes and sabotage threatened the security of the war industries, military installations, and major transportation and population centers of other regions.

Initially, only a few thousand Axis POWs had been brought over to the United States from Europe, but after the Allied forces defeated Rommel's troops in North Africa in May 1943, more than 300,000 soldiers were taken prisoner. Thousands more were taken captive after the invasion of Normandy a year later. What to do with these large numbers of POWs was now a logistical and urgent problem.

The United States, an ocean away from the fighting, seemed the only place to house and oversee such a large population of enemy soldiers. Empty transport ships were pressed into service, removing the prisoners from the front lines and delivering them to American soil through ports of entry in Boston, New York, and Norfolk. Some 115,000 German POWs began pouring in. Eventually, more than 400,000 German, Italian, and Japanese POWs were interned in the United States during the years 1943–46.

The U.S. Army Provost Marshal General's Office directed the POW effort, sending the captives primarily west and south. Their policies conformed to the agreement outlined in the 1929 Geneva Convention on the Treatment of Prisoners of War requiring humane treatment to include adequate food, shelter, and health care. Enlisted POWs were required to work for their captors but were paid a stipend. Noncommissioned officers were required to supervise work details, and nothing was demanded of officers, yet they were to receive the same compensation as before their capture. These rules were strictly adhered to in the hopes that American POWs held in Germany would receive the same humane treatment. Regular inspections took place, conducted by international, neutral observers such as the Swiss and the Red Cross, to assure the fulfillment of these obligations.

Since the Southeast had been identified as an ideal location, several large camps were built in Alabama (Camp Aliceville), North Carolina (Camps Butner and Sutton), Tennessee (Camp Forrest), and Georgia (Camp Gordon), each housing several thousand Germans and a smaller number of Italians. By the spring of 1944, South Carolina had built five satellite camps for the internment of several hundred prisoners at each site under the direction of the larger neighboring state camps. These subcamps were located at Aiken, Columbia, Spartanburg, Hampton, and Charleston for the purpose of using the manpower to assist with the agricultural harvests and timber industry. Six months later additional camps were organized at Barnwell, Myrtle Beach, Columbia, and Walterboro. By July 1945 more installations were set up in rural locations around the state at Bennettsville, Camden, Greenwood, Florence, Sumter, Holly Hill, Whitmire, Witherbee, York, and, later, Norway; and all the South Carolina camps, with the exception of Camp Croft in Spartanburg (by now an autonomous base camp), came under the direction of Fort Jackson, centrally located in Columbia.

Often the large camps occupied vacant barracks of nearby military facilities or former New Deal Civilian Conservation Corps camps built by the government for displaced workers of the Great Depression. The smaller installations were made up of tentlike temporary structures with wooden floors. The typical compound was surrounded by barbed wire stockade fencing with four or more corner watchtowers. The more permanent camps might include recreational facilities such as soccer fields and volleyball courts. Fort Jackson and Camp Croft prisoners had more opportunity for entertainment and diversion with musical performances and plays performed by prisoners on POW-built stages. The prisoners published camp newspapers, reporting both camp and war news, but under American censorship. Even night classes in English, history, and mathematics were offered, taught by POWs from German universities. The inmates were allowed their own cooks to prepare their provisions suitable for German tastes. Another privilege in some camps was a POW-run prison store, where their comrades could purchase beer, candy, cigarettes and other small articles with chits from their earned wages.

On occasion, when Americans got wind of these prison-camp privileges, they felt that the enemy, interned in their own backyard, was living better than they were, especially considering the staple rationing they were enduring. Some of the camps were better organized than others, however, and living conditions varied. Several overcrowded ones did not have enough latrines or showers, creating problems in sanitation; one inspector, in his report, even warned of the possibility of a major epidemic outbreak. The tent housing often leaked, creating more health and cleanliness concerns. And in the spring of 1945, when Americans learned of the concentration-camp atrocities in Germany and, later, when Germany surrendered, food and privileges were significantly cut back. In some cases the food ration was less than 1,000 calories per day, and the variety declined also. One report notes the same bean soup served for lunch every day for eight weeks at the Shaw Field Camp in Sumter.

Working conditions for the POWs were varied as well. All were expected to maintain their compounds without compensation, and although outside work was considered "voluntary," American camp commanders ruled that prisoners who didn't work, didn't eat. The majority of the South Carolina POWs were employed in the pulpwood or agricultural industries, as South Carolina farmers faced a serious manpower shortage, especially at harvest time. Potential employers had to navigate the government's red tape and establish proof that sufficient local labor was not available in order to hire POW labor. If they were successful, they paid the U.S. government $3.50 per day for each prisoner, which helped defray the camp expenses for food and housing. The men received 80 cents per day of this fee in credits that could be held in reserve until the end of the war or spent in the camp canteen.

Initially, the people of the smaller farming communities were frightened by the prospect of enemy soldiers in their towns, but soon a demand for labor—and curiosity—took over. A group of 200 inmates was sent to Bamberg and Orangeburg Counties in the fall of 1943 to work the peanut harvest. Hundreds of onlookers drove by to see the enemy at work in their fields. A Bennettsville man remarked that the prisoners employed on his father's Marlboro County cotton farm were some of the best, most disciplined workers he had ever had. Many other farmers gave similar praise. A heartier lunch (than the one that was sent along by the camp), and even a daily can of beer provided by some employers, may have been an added incentive for these foreign workers. One prisoner remembered a barbecue after the day's work on an Edgefield farm.

Working conditions on the farms, however, could be strenuous especially in the hot, humid, insect-infested Carolina summers. The pulp-and-paper industry working conditions were more rigorous still; timber work could be dangerous and also required more training. The language barrier often prevented adequate communication and instruction, and stringent production quotas kept the POW's working at a grueling pace. In some instances if the quota was not met, workers would be put in isolation back at the camp and denied the chance to wash up from the day's exertion. A letter from one of these prisoners expresses his belief that some South Carolina employers exploited their captive labor force well beyond their contractual agreements. Whatever the POW experience, South

Carolina farmers used this cheap labor as long as they could to maintain and harvest the state's major cash crops of peanuts, cotton, and peaches.

At the war's end several politicians called for a speedy return to Germany of the more than 8,000 POWs in South Carolina. They thought it vital to open up the civilian jobs to accommodate the returning American GIs. The farmers quickly protested, because they realized that bringing home the GIs would take many months and labor remained scarce. As much as a year later, many prisoners were still in the state, filling the labor gap until the camps were closed. The last POWs were shipped home in July 1946.

These days the strange story of the Nazi prisoners of war in South Carolina is largely forgotten, but it tells of a significant, if brief, interlude in the state's history. Although there were more than 2,200 escape attempts from Nazi POW camps scattered across the United States during World War II, the day-to-day life of the vast majority of prisoners was relatively uneventful. But their presence in our own backyard brought South Carolinians face to face with an enemy from a war on another continent, exposing them to an ever more important global perspective. And this experience led them to adapt to their unusual, dual role of captor and employer, while successfully maintaining the agricultural productivity of the state and contributing to the American war effort.

All That Business between the Sheets

·1948·

The memo from the South Carolina textile magnate to his advertising agency in New York was typically short and to the point—like all communiqués from the flamboyant Col. Elliot Springs:

> Get me a picture of a girl in an enameled iron bed, with the enamel knocked off, with a hole in the plaster behind her, a dirty barbershop calendar above the bed, a bureau with a cracked mirror, and badly wrinkled sheets with holes in them. Put a cigarette in the girl's mouth, rumple her hair, and let the caption be, I LOVE THESE SLOWBURNING SPRINGMAID SHEETS.
>
> Make sure you get a release from the model, her husband, the photographer, and their lawyers because all the advertising agents in the country are going to be sore at me. They may have to think up a new ad.
>
> Yours,
> Elliot Springs

A writer for *Printer's Ink*, one of the advertising industry's major trade journals, was more than "sore." He called the ad campaign launched in 1948 by the Fort Mill, South Carolina, textile manufacturer "the most flagrant current example of bad taste we have with us today." Other equally shocked industry insiders echoed his scathing review.

Perhaps the most famous, or infamous, Springmaid ad in the series showed a man in Indian headdress casting a weary glance up at a smiling, miniskirted Indian woman stepping out of their (presumably shared) bedsheet hammock. The headline read: "A BUCK WELL SPENT ON A SPRINGMAID SHEET." Although the body copy of the ad actually touted the financial wisdom of investing in the Springmaid product, the provocative illustration was clearly suggestive. *Life* magazine refused to run the ad in 1950, as did *Family Circle*.

Elliot Springs, or "the Colonel," as he was called in deference to his daring exploits as a World War I flying ace, was unfazed by all this criticism over his ads. In fact he delighted in tweaking the eastern, Ivy League advertising establishment. He received thousands of outraged letters from ministers, college professors, ladies' club members, and Sunday-school teachers—outraged by the ads' headlines. He relished each and every one of them, and he even published some in the Springs Mill company newsletter.

To the Colonel his ads had nothing to do with good taste or what might be offensive to some groups of people. He had a job to do. He was selling sheets and brand-name recognition for his company. If he had to break new ground in marketing history while he was at it, so be it; that was just part of his job.

When Elliot Springs took over the family's textile mills following the death of his father, it was 1931, the bottom of the Great Depression. The textile industry in South Carolina was in deep trouble. Although Springs Cotton Mills had been formed in 1887, when Fort Mill was hardly more than a crossroads amid the upstate's cotton fields, it had survived into the 1930s only by negotiating a perilous course through a series of mergers and desperate corporate maneuvers. It barely struggled along until the market suddenly boomed with the advent of World War I. Overnight, the government needed vast amounts of cotton cloth for (among other things) bed sheets. Springs Cotton Mills responded with a major expansion in their manufacturing capacity to meet this wartime demand. But the stock market crash in 1929 left the company overbuilt and now in a more precarious position than ever.

In those days all sheets were sold in retail stores as "flat goods;" all sheets were flat sheets. Fitted, bottom sheets were still products of the future. The flat sheets were manufactured, packaged, and sold to retailers one dozen to a package. They were all white, all cotton, and all stacked on a shelf in the store to be sold as customers called for them, one or two at a time. Because all sheets were more or less alike, retailers dealt with them as "loss leaders," merchandise carried essentially to attract customers but not necessarily expected to be a high-profit item.

Elliott Springs understood that if he wanted more business—if he wanted to create greater demand for his sheets—he needed to make customers more aware of his product. He needed something to capture their attention, not just the attention of retailers who would order cotton sheets in bulk but that of housewives who would ask for Springmaid sheets by name. Better yet, if he could gain a little notoriety for his brand name, the quicker that name recognition would translate into company profits.

In 1948 the Colonel hired John Brooks to launch and manage a bold, new marketing plan, but Springs wrote much of the advertising copy himself. He claimed that he was spoofing advertising, although he actually was wielding the medium's considerable power with great skill.

Another example of the Colonel's originality was an ad that featured a group of young firemen positioned below the window of a burning house. They're holding an outstretched bed sheet, into which is falling a lovely young woman who has jumped to safety from above, her skirts flying high above her waist. The headline reads: "WE LOVE TO CATCH THEM ON A SPRINGMAID SHEET."

The accompanying body copy of the ad is written in rhyme, with tongue firmly held in cheek: "We love to give the gals a treat and catch them on a Springmaid sheet. We make them, Sir—and that's no jest. The sheets, we mean. They'll pass the test."

If the advertising copywriters in New York weren't impressed, they had to concede that the campaign made a positive impression on a very conservative (if not repressed) 1950s general public. The ribald and irreverent ads achieved the brand-name recognition Elliott Springs wanted, and total sales for Springs Mills, Inc., more than doubled between 1948 and 1962. There were some sixty different ads that ran during a twenty-year period; they were mostly centered around some leggy, buxom, scantily-attired young woman.

In the late 1940s Springmaid introduced a new product—percale sheets, a better-quality product with a higher thread content. About that time the Colonel dispensed with the calendar art and used actual photos of the "prominent hostess of New York and Paris, Gypsy Rose Lee," who claimed, "MY FAVORITE NIGHTSPOT IS A SPRINGMADE CANDYCALE SHEET." These "Candycale" sheets were pin-striped in pastel colors, like candy. He introduced solid pastels as well, along with floral prints such as "Princess Rose" and "Fresh Daisies."

The only specialty sheets made prior to this were mostly gift items—sheets printed in a Christmas theme—which only had limited, seasonal appeal. Now Springmaid changed its packaging to a see-through cellophane wrapper, two sheets to a package with colorful printing on the outside. Suddenly, everyone wanted fashionable bed linens, and Springs Mills moved into the industry forefront and eventually took dominant position in the field. Eventually, the name of the patterns became so important to consumers that the manufacturer's name became secondary. Springs Mills met this challenge by hiring outside fashion designers like Emilio Pucci (in 1966) and Bill Blass (in 1970) to come up with fresh, new patterns and colors for the high-fashion, "designer" bedroom.

As for the risqué ad campaign, it was discontinued about a year after Colonel Springs's death in 1959. William Kirk, who for twenty years was a marketing executive with Springs Industries, Inc., explained that the series had run its course and done its job by then. "Toward the end of the campaign," he said, "the ads weren't that funny and they were appearing in such unlikely magazines as *Popular Mechanics* and *Field and Stream* . . . the bulk of whose readership was hardly the home-making audience Springs wanted to reach."

The mentality of the consumer had shifted to a more sophisticated level, so Springs's advertising shifted with them. Starting in the 1960s, ads for Springmaid appeared in *Better Homes and Gardens*, *Southern Living*, and *House Beautiful*. They depicted fashionable bedrooms handsomely accented with color-coordinated sheets and pillow cases by Springmaid, with no people shown at all. The psychological trick, here, was to invite the consumer to "see themselves" in this attractive picture. Though this approach was certainly more mainstream than "A Buck Well Spent," it was nonetheless effective.

In the early 1980s Springs Mills was the nation's fourth-largest publicly held textile company, with annual sales of $917 million. It was also one of the state's largest employers—a far cry from the start-up cotton mill of 1887 built to try and shake off the economic doldrums of Reconstruction and bring the promise of new business to upstate South Carolina.

The Legend of the Gray Man

· 1954 ·

Bill Collins was never what you'd call an unreasonable man, never prone to any particular flights of fantasy or silly romantic legends. In the fall of 1954, he was preoccupied with the end-of-season sales figures for his Georgetown, South Carolina, car dealership, thinking more about the sales incentives for the new model year just unveiled and the latest directives from the big bosses up in Detroit. With all that on his mind, he was only vaguely aware of the weather reports warning about a sizable storm brewing in the West Indies, which was heading toward the South Carolina coast.

In the mid-1950s hurricane prediction was still fairly primitive. Weather forecasters were largely dependent on barometer readings from outposts in the Caribbean, reports coming in from military ships out at sea, and the innate wisdom of enlightened experience and instinct. Bill Collins knew what everyone along the Eastern seaboard knew—that violent storms are always a possibility during the five long months of hurricane season. This year was no different.

That Friday, October 15, everyone along the Carolina coast was keeping one ear on the radio and an eye toward the sky. The weather report was sounding more ominous with every passing hour. Saturday was dismal, with intermittent rain and vicious wind whipping the small island mercilessly. Storm warnings were a normal part of "beach life," and Collins knew it was wise to take them seriously when things got to a certain point. He owned a beach house on nearby Pawleys Island, which had been in the family for generations. Spending summers there had been an important part of his childhood, and it was an important part of his family life as an adult as well. Heeding the radio warnings, he closed the dealership in Georgetown and with his wife headed north toward Pawleys and the beach house to take a few precautions—just in case.

Arriving on the island, they shuttered the windows and packed away the outdoor things that could catch the wind. It was the same routine they went through every hurricane season when things started looking bad. The preparation took only a couple of hours. They even planned to stay the night, as there was no real cause for alarm. Nothing indicated this was going to be different from any of the other "close calls" that came with owning South Carolina beachfront property this time of year.

Just before dusk, however, Collins had a strange impulse. He told his wife he'd be back shortly, and he walked out to something the family always called "the lookout," a small gazebo built on a high dune connected to the house by a long, weathered boardwalk. He stood there in the twilight—the surf whipped into a fine mist by the strong offshore wind. He looked up and down the beach. It was totally deserted. Not only was the weather uninviting, it was late fall now, and all the tourists had vacated the island for the season. Collins didn't even see lights from any of the "old-timer's" cottages—year-round beach houses he'd known all his life, places that had survived a dozen bad storms. What happened next to Bill Collins is hard to explain.

From his position high on the dune, Collins had a sweeping view of the entire beach. Even at this hour, at dusk and under gathering clouds, Collins could make out the figure of a man walking toward him, dressed in gray clothing. The man seemed to walk with a deliberate gait as if he were on a purposeful mission, hurrying to tell someone important news. Just as Collins focused his startled gaze, the man suddenly disappeared. At that very moment Collins knew he had seen the Gray Man.

The legend of the Gray Man originated during South Carolina's plantation days of the early 1800s. It is the tragic story of a wealthy young man who returned to his coastal plantation after having spent two years being schooled abroad. Hurrying along the Pawleys Island strand mounted on his fine horse, with his faithful servant following behind, he was going to visit his fiancée in residence at her family's beach home there. In his rush to meet with his lovely lady, the young man spied what he thought was a shortcut through the lowlands that surrounded Middleton Pond. He suddenly reigned his horse onto the narrow pathway leading from the beach, and for a while, he seemed to be making good time. Suddenly, his horse stumbled and fell, and the young man was thrown into the marsh. The horse whinnied and struggled but could not find its footing. It had landed in a hidden mire of quicksand, and, sadly, its master was also caught in the sinking pool, as well. The young man desperately reached out and struggled to grasp for any branch or tree root, but he just sank farther into the mire. Only his servant, following several paces behind, heard his screams. Although the servant tried desperately to save his master, the situation was hopeless. Horrified by the tragedy he'd just witnessed, the servant rode back with devastating news for the young woman awaiting her fiancé—that he'd been lost forever in the quicksand.

So grief stricken was the young maiden that she simply could not be consoled. Her father carried her upstairs to bed and summoned a physician. There she remained sequestered for several days, unable even to attend the funeral for her beloved. Only after repeated, strenuous pleas from her parents did she agree to dress and go for a solitary walk along the beach. They hoped that by doing this, she might regain her strength.

As she was walking along the sandy tideline in the evening twilight, suddenly the gaunt figure of her lost love, dressed in a dark-gray suit, appeared before her. She ran toward him, desperate to behold his handsome face. But just as she did, he disappeared into the evening mist. As she recounted this amazing story to her disbelieving family, she insisted that her fiancé seemed to be beckoning to her, calling for her to leave the island. She said he seemed to be warning of some unknown danger to her and her family. So strong was this encounter with her deceased lover that she actually convinced her family to leave Pawleys Island for the safety of their inland plantation home. They knew not what danger they might be avoiding, but her experience was so vivid, they couldn't deny her ardent pleas.

The family fled the island in the early hours of the following day. Then, that night as they were resting from their journey in the familiar safety of their inland home, a fierce hurricane descended upon Pawleys Island. The storm destroyed most of the island's buildings, save the family beach home of the young woman whose lover had been lost.

More than a century later, the story of the Gray Man, with his warning of a pending storm, lives on in the hearts and minds of Lowcountry residents. They claim he still returns. They say he brings dire warning of a hurricane's advancing wrath to those lucky enough to see him.

According to residents living on Pawleys Island, the Gray Man appeared again in 1893. As coastal skies grew darker and the winds more insistent, people told of seeing a man of medium height and slight build walking on the beach. All of his clothing was gray, even his hat. No one could see his face or identify this mysterious individual because of the fading light and the shadows that were falling over the sands. But those who saw him warned families and friends, and they all promptly left the island.

Later that same day a hurricane struck with savage fury. Several large beach homes on the north end of the island and most of two rows of huge sand dunes disappeared into the waves before the night was over. Nearby, at Magnolia Beach where the Gray Man was not seen, an entire village of summer homes washed out to sea, causing the tragic loss of many lives.

Does the ghost of the Gray Man still walk the beach of Pawleys Island? Does he still warn people of disastrous hurricanes heading their way? Some are believers; others are not. But many are the people in South Carolina who don't hesitate to evacuate the coast whenever there's a sighting of a man in gray walking along Pawleys Island beach—especially under leaden skies.

Of course, Bill Collins had heard the legend of the Gray Man as a child. Every kid growing up along this coast knows the story. But Collins had long ago outgrown his belief in ghost stories. As the phantom appeared and disappeared in front of his eyes, he became a true believer that October evening back in 1954. He gathered up his family and left Pawleys Island that very night. Shortly after he did, Hurricane Hazel thundered ashore, washing houses and dunes into the angry sea. Somehow, though, amid this terrible destruction, Collins's house stood untouched. Newspaper accounts at the time quoted the incredulous car dealer as saying, "Not even my [rooftop] TV antenna blew down." He remained forever grateful to the Gray Man and his warning.

If the weather forecasts start sounding ominous along the South Carolina coast, and you hear of a Gray Man seen striding along the beach of Pawleys Island . . . what will *you* do?

South Carolina's Lady Olympian

· 1961 ·

She stood tall as ever as she rose from her seat on the dais of honor and started toward the podium, and the entire room erupted in spontaneous cheers and applause. The lanky woman being honored this night had waited a long time to hear her name called as an inductee to the South Carolina Sports Hall of Fame. She stepped up to the microphone and made a short, typically modest acceptance speech and then returned to her seat. "Ludy," as she was called, always packed plenty of wit; but she was never long on words. Still, the poignancy of this long-overdue moment, however short, wasn't lost on the sports luminaries assembled there. This was Lucile Ellerbe Godbold, the first woman athlete ever to be so honored in South Carolina's Sports Hall of Fame. She was the state's first female Olympic champion and an international legend in the world of women's track-and-field competition.

The thirty-nine years between her defining moment as an unlikely Olympian in the 1922 Paris Games and her election to the Hall of Fame were spent in service to her two primary passions: women's athletics and teaching. "The longer I teach," she once said, "the better teacher I become." The honor she was receiving this night was coming at the zenith of her fifty-eight-year career in women's physical education.

The career of Ludy Godbold evolved from inauspicious

beginnings. She was born on May 31, 1900, in Marion, South Carolina. She moved around the state with her family several times before she entered elementary school, living in McColl and then in Wagener before the family finally settled in Estill, which she always officially listed as her "hometown." She was tall and thin—never a great beauty—and didn't actually discover her innate athletic talent until she entered Winthrop College in the fall of 1918. There, she had access to physical education classes, a gymnasium, and sports equipment never available to her before.

The concept of women participating in organized athletics was not universally accepted in Ludy's day, especially in the American South. Women were supposed to accept their societal roles as wives and mothers, leaving the overt feats of skill and strength to men. Many educators felt that the competitive nature of track and field, in particular, might be actually dangerous to women—physically and emotionally. One physician was quoted as saying, "The adolescent girl who is subjected to highly emotional situations is but sowing the seeds of a nervous breakdown [later in life] . . . by putting undue stress on the endocrine glands."

At Winthrop College, however, a slightly more enlightened attitude prevailed. Ruth Bartlett, the school's director of physical education, encouraged Ludy to participate in the annual spring track meet. There, to everyone's surprise, she broke three American records—in the discus throw, the shot put, and the hop-step-jump. This stunned the crowd as well as the organizers of the meet. Who *was* this amazing girl from Estill?

Miss Bartlett encouraged Ludy to travel to Mamaroneck, New York, where tryouts were being held for positions on the United States Olympic team. This was the first time any woman athlete in South Carolina—or in Ludy's life, for that matter—had ever suggested reaching for anything as lofty as an Olympic goal. In a spontaneous burst of enthusiasm and support, Ludy's classmates raised the money to send her to New

York, where she did not disappoint them.

On May 13, 1922, the Eastern Qualifying Meet took place at Oaksmere School in Mamaroneck. Participating that Saturday was the largest group of women athletes ever assembled at a track-and-field competition in the history of the United States. Although few people realized it at the time, this was a turning point for women's athletics in America. There were girls from schools and colleges stretching from Maine to Florida, 102 athletes in all. Ludy and one other girl, Margaret Kennedy, represented Winthrop. By association they were representing South Carolina, as well.

The girls watched in quiet amusement as the other contestants were groomed and fawned over by coaches and trainers, who rubbed them down with special elixirs and unguents. After each event these "coaches" would rush up to the girls and cover their shoulders with blankets for a proper "cool down." Ludy and Margaret were on their own, but it didn't seem to hurt their performance in any way. Ludy won the basketball-throw event with a toss of 88 feet, 3.25 inches. She placed second in the 100-yard dash, and set the world's record in the one-hand, 8-pound shot-put throw with 35 feet, 11 inches!

Meanwhile, back at Winthrop, all the girls waited anxiously for news from New York. On May 15 Dr. David B. Johnson, president of Winthrop, addressed the student body assembled for the Monday morning chapel service. He held up a telegram from the head of the National Women's Track Athletics Committee and read it aloud: "Miss Godbold chosen for Paris. . . . Have her practice shot put with both hands, also 300-yard dash, 1,000 yard run. Congratulations." The room exploded in cheers.

Ludy spent the following summer at Winthrop, training hard for the upcoming games. This was completely new ground. Back in 1896, when Baron Pierre de Coubertin revived the ancient tradition of Olympic Games, he did not envision competition for women. Although special events involving women were gradually added, these displays were more like exhibitions than sanctioned competitions. First to break through the sex barrier was a demonstration of women's golf in 1900, although a medal was only awarded to the winner posthumously, half a century later! In 1908 tennis was added; then came archery and, finally, figure skating. These exhibitions eventually included swimming, diving, and gymnastics. But the officially sanctioned sports available to women always varied from one Olympics to the next. Standardized women's competition between nations proved elusive until the Paris Games of 1922. Even then, the athletes would compete under the Olympic subtitle of The International Track Meet for Women.

As the date for the Olympic Games approached, once more Ludy's classmates were pressed into service with a fundraising campaign to help send her to Paris. This they did willingly, and Ludy was officially listed as one of the thirteen women on the United States Olympic team. On August 1, 1922, she sailed for France aboard the *Aquitania* with first-class accommodations and special permission to train on deck for an hour each morning and in the ship's gymnasium, which was reserved for practice every afternoon.

Ludy was under an incredible amount of pressure to perform well in the Games. Winthrop's president, Dr. Johnson, was en route to Paris to watch the competition. Newspapers quoted him as saying, "Everyone's expectation of victory rests on Lucile Godbold."

Even Ludy's mother wrote her the following advice, "Enter everything you think you can win. Remember you want the individual score as well as the American record."

The events were held on Sunday, August 20, 1922, as a crowd of 20,000 (many of them Americans) filed expectantly into Pershing Stadium. Seventy-seven women—from Great Britain, France, Czechoslovakia, Switzerland, and the United States—were entered in eleven official events plus four demonstration contests. The United States team faced women who had experienced international competition before. Among these was the French woman who owned the world's record in the shot put circle at a little more than 18 meters.

As Ludy stepped up and prepared to throw, her coach shouted, "Now, ol' South Carolina Mountaineer, show 'em what the South can do!" What she did was throw "the pill" beyond 22 meters, establishing a new world record. Ludy Godbold had just become the first woman to win an Olympic gold medal. The American flag was raised, and the national anthem rang out—twice. Reporters and photographers descended on the field, and celebration rained down on everyone there.

After her amazing victory in the shot-put circle, Ludy went on to win the hop-step-jump event as well. She placed second in the basketball throw plus the 300-meter race. She won third in both the javelin throw and the 1,000-meter run. No other woman in the world had approached this level of performance on the Olympic field. Ludy earned an astonishing 18 points and brought home a world record of six medals to a grateful nation.

In South Carolina she was widely hailed as a heroine, but her goal was not to gain notoriety or become a celebrity. Even before the Olympic Games, Ludy had agreed to accept a position as director of physical education at Columbia College to teach—and that's exactly where she went. There she stayed for the next fifty-eight productive years, expanding the sports opportunities for women athletes and heightening the awareness of physical education as a viable, fulfilling career.

Many honors came her way after her triumph at the 1922 Olympic Games. Her election to the South Carolina Sports Hall of Fame in 1961 was among her favorites. But Lucile Godbold's focus remained on teaching and expanding the opportunities for women's athletics in America. She died in 1981 and rests "back home" in Estill near a handsome monument erected in her honor.

Hugo's Wrath
· 1989 ·

As the night of September 21 unfolded, some 400 souls were huddled in Lincoln High School in McClellanville, South Carolina, seeking refuge. The building had been officially designated as a "safe" storm shelter, and what was almost the entire population of the town had just settled in for what they hoped would be only a moderately uncomfortable night. The families gathered there felt excitement, to be sure. And dread. And worry. But the primary concern was getting the children and older people settled in as comfortably as possible. To that end people were scattered with makeshift bedding throughout the building in various hallways and classrooms.

Just after 10:00 P.M., torrents of rain started pounding down on the flat roof of the single-story structure, announcing the arrival of the storm. Not long after the rain began, all the lights went out, plunging the shelter into total darkness. The winds whipped up, escalating into a screaming furor. Suddenly, everyone heard a strange, rushing noise above the already fierce roar of the storm.

In the pitch-black night, as the storm center pushed violently over peninsular Charleston some 35 miles to the south, the accompanying tidal surge rushed in on McClellanville with horrendous force and speed. The cold, black water of Hugo's surge rushed in from everywhere, pinning the exit doors shut and turning the school into a nightmarish death trap. The frightened throng was divided among the various classrooms, cafeteria, band room, and gym.

Jennings Austin, principal of Lincoln High, described the terrifying scene. "Water was about eye level and going up. I managed to get one classroom open. It was dark, but I knew the teacher's desk was in the corner, so we climbed on that and broke out the Plexiglas window so we could get out on the roof." Austin and Charlie DuTart, a deputy sheriff, helped others out the window and onto the roof, where they had to hold on with all their strength against the 135-mph wind. In the darkness DuTart had only the illuminated dial of his wristwatch to mark the passing of time.

"We cried. We were angry," said DuTart. "We must have looked at the time every two minutes for the five and a half hours we were up there. We tried to judge how high the water was. The way we could was by seeing the cars floating by." At the same time DuTart and Austin feared for the safety of the rest of the townspeople, who were stranded in other parts of the school building. They knew that several hundred were in the cafeteria. Those evacuees were scrambling onto chairs and tabletops to keep their heads above the rising water.

In the classrooms many of the adults were shoving out the ceiling tiles to lift small children up through the openings as high as possible away from the onrushing waters. Some people scrambled onto the bleachers in the gymnasium as the waters quickly climbed after them. Others crowded up onto the school's stage and held their children over their heads as the water rose up to their chests. They sang and prayed, cried, and comforted one another throughout the seemingly endless night. Finally, the water level peaked at just a little more than 7 feet and then slowly began to recede.

The many heroes of the disaster and their exhausted comrades miraculously cheated death. No one perished at Lincoln High in what could easily have been a disaster costing hundreds of lives.

The irony of this story is that it was a hurricane that gave McClellanville its *start*. The sleepy old fishing village of

McClellanville, nestled among the live oaks along Jeremy Creek, was at one time the summer haven for nineteenth-century rice planters who lived along the Santee River. The beginnings of the existing village date back to the mid-1800s, when the planters built retreats here, away from the disease-ridden backwater plantations. Another devastating hurricane, back in 1822, had completely wiped out a village of planter homes on nearby Cedar Island, and the new site was thought to be safer from storms. These South Santee planters began purchasing lots on Jeremy Creek and constructing new summer homes there. After the Civil War the punitive economic policies of Reconstruction forced some of the area planters to completely abandon their large plantations and move to the little summer village on a permanent basis.

In the 1920s McClellanville became one of the first places in the state where shrimpers from the west coast of Florida would come to trawl the rich coastal waters. Eventually, the town developed into one of the major fishing ports in the state. But the day after Hugo, McClellanville's future as a fishing port was in question. It appeared that this hurricane called Hugo was now bringing McClellanville to an *end*.

Most of the fleet of large shrimp boats had been tossed about like toys in a bathtub and left marooned on the landscape. Cars and pleasure boats were upended, overturned, and shuffled like playing cards. Trees were uprooted, others snapped in half. Roads were obstructed and access to buildings blocked. Even caskets from some of the old churchyards were set adrift, compounding this grim and bewildering scene. Many homes and businesses were completely destroyed, and the whole town was covered in layers of "pluff" mud, debris, and dead fish while a pervasive, foul stench hung in the air. One resident returned home to find a decaying pelican spread across her dining-room table. For days the town was cut off from any relief efforts because of the massive flooding. Eventually help got through, and the long, dreary, and frustrating process of cleaning and rebuilding began.

Across the rest of the state, this Category Four hurricane (defined as winds of 131–155 mph with storm surge 13–18 feet above normal) left a widespread trail of destruction churning from the Lowcountry up through the Midlands and into the Pee Dee areas. Loss of life in South Carolina numbered twenty-eight deaths as a direct result of the storm, although as many as fifty-six deaths are counted as storm related (including a heart-attack victim in the aftermath of the flooding at Lincoln High School). This relatively low loss of human life for a storm of this magnitude was attributed to a successful evacuation and response to the hurricane threat.

The catastrophic impact on the state's economy was extensive and profound. The statistics tell the story. An esti-mated 23,000 homes were severely damaged or destroyed, leaving 64,000 people homeless and seeking temporary shelter. An estimated 200,000 to 300,000 were left without employment. More than 10,000 miles of secondary roads were impaired. The Department of Education estimated more than $55 million in property damage to the South Carolina school systems. Clemson University research showed damages in excess of $322 million to the agricultural industry. The forest industry in particular lost more than 6.7 billion board feet of lumber (enough to build 660,000 homes), valued at $1.04 billion. The loss of timber represented more than 36 percent of the state's entire woodland, and reforestation efforts were predicted to take at least fifty years.

The economic staple industries of fishing, tourism, mili-tary, and government suffered losses that were felt for years afterward as well. In addition to these losses in South Carolina, Hugo caused another $1 billion in damages as it made its way through North Carolina and another $50 million in Virginia, with thirteen hurricane-related deaths in those two states. Prior to its landfall in the United States, the storm wreaked havoc across the Caribbean, causing severe destruction in the British and U.S. Virgin Islands and Puerto Rico.

And what became of the quaint village of McClellanville? At present it is remarkably recovered. The old buildings continue to reflect the architectural evolution of the town from a summer retreat for plantation families to a thriving, incorporated municipality. The community takes renewed pride in its restored residential, commercial, religious, and educational properties, which date from the 1860s to the 1930s.

And lest anyone forget—a small plaque has been placed on a wall near the cafeteria door in McClellanville's Lincoln High School. It's placed a little more than 6 feet above the floor, showing how high the storm water rose that night. But no 8-by-10-inch plaque can measure the level of fear experienced by the people who had gathered at the school for shelter against Hugo's wrath. Nor can it measure the brave and courageous spirit of the residents who miraculously survived and later went on to rebuild their lives.

Afterward, as a result of the severe flooding and the 17.2-foot tidal surge, Lincoln High School was removed from the list of evacuation sites, and no shelters are now located east of U.S. Highway 17.

The Return of the
H. L. Hunley
· 2000 ·

In the stifling heat and humidity that hovers over Charleston every August, things around town appeared to be quite normal. Business in the Holy City during the millennium year was booming. Downtown was crowded with the usual mix of tourists. Traffic on the old Cooper River Bridge slowed to its regular crawl at rush hour. And speculation in the local real-estate market continued at an all-time high.

The mood in Charleston couldn't have been sharper in its contrast to those grim, final days of the Civil War, when "the cause" was clearly lost and pre-war memories of grace and glory were fading into distant memory. Time and perspective had taught Charleston a great deal since 1864. Few would argue that the present is indeed Charleston's true Golden Age, not the heavily romanticized days before the war, when slavery-driven wealth covered the city in a deceiving veneer of affluence and architectural sophistication.

But at exactly 8:39 A.M., on August 8, 2000, something broke the surface of the choppy Atlantic about 4 miles outside Charleston Harbor that suddenly closed the historic gap between *then* and *now*. The mighty crane's engine hesitated for a moment on its massive floating barge. The sound grew deeper and more urgent. With ocean swells rolling at twenty-eight-second intervals, the actual moment of transition from sea to air was high risk for this fragile relic of the past. Then suddenly, a cheer went up from the informal escort fleet of VIP boats and pleasure craft assembled to witness the event. With hundreds of cameras and the whole world watching, the crane hoisted into the hazy August day a lost treasure of the Confederacy, the *H. L. Hunley*.

She was a miracle of maritime technology in 1864 when, as the first submarine in history to sink an enemy ship, she stealthily ambushed and sank the Yankee sloop *U.S.S. Housatonic* and then unaccountably vanished for 131 long years. With her disappeared a crew of eight Confederate volunteers. And thus, she entered the realm of heroic legend, shrouded in the mystery and human tragedy that always surround war. But on this day, history had been recovered. At last the *Hunley* was coming "home."

The *Hunley* was built in the spring of 1863 in Mobile, Alabama, and sent by train to Charleston for crew training and sea trials. With new technology and inexperience came tragic blunders, and the first attempts to use her ended badly. Five members of her first crew drowned when an operator caused the sub to dive before the hatches were secured. Shortly thereafter, another crew—this time eight—perished when a flood valve was inadvertently left open. Almost every man who ever climbed aboard the *Hunley* died. Some of the sailors along the Charleston waterfront dubbed her the "murdering machine."

General P. G. T. Beauregard, who was commanding efforts to break the Union blockade that was literally starving Charleston at the time, was horrified at the specter that eventually greeted the vessel's salvors after its second failure. He later wrote in his memoirs, "[It was] indescribably ghastly. The unfortunate men were contorted into all kinds of horrible attitudes . . . and the blackened faces of all presented the expression of their despair and agony."

Thereafter, Beauregard issued strict orders that all future crew recruits be made fully aware of the "desperately hazardous nature of the service required." Even though the odds of success for another mission were duly measured, the blockade's stranglehold on Charleston was inflicting enormous hardship on soldiers and citizens alike. So many sailors volunteered to give the *Hunley* another try that a new commander, Lt. George Dixon, was able to choose the cream of the crop.

Crude as she was, the 40-foot-long *Hunley* was a sleek and formidable weapon. Her existence was supposedly a secret, but Rebel deserters had spread rumors among the Union navy of some terrible new "infernal Confederate machine." In response, the Yankee fleet of ironclads enforcing the blockage deployed a complicated network of underwater chains, which effectively foiled all plans to use the *Hunley* within the harbor.

Dixon was forced to redirect his efforts toward the larger wooden ships anchored several miles offshore. Almost nightly for nearly a month, the crew struggled out to sea in search of a target, only to return exhausted by the limits of physical energy and the protective cover of darkness. Finally, on February 17, shortly after sunset, the *Hunley*'s crew of eight squeezed inside the cramped crew cabin (only 4 feet high and 3½ feet wide) and slipped away from her dock on nearby Sullivan's Island. The men took their positions sitting along a hand-turned crankshaft that was linked to a propeller outside the iron hull. Two snorkel pipes and a set of leather bellows pulled air into the sub, but only when it was near the surface. The *Hunley* traveled submerged at a depth of about 6 feet. Dixon navigated by compass and surfaced at regular intervals to identify targets through a viewport in the forward hatch. The only light inside the tiny sub was a single candle.

The *Housatonic* was a wooden-hulled steam sloop that on this night had strayed within striking distance of the *Hunley*. She was nearly 5.5 miles east-south-east of Fort Sumter. The known facts about what happened next are a matter of record. At 8:45 P.M., a sailor aboard the *Housatonic* noticed something strange in the water off the starboard bow. At first he thought it was a large porpoise or a floating log; then he knew he was wrong. He sounded the alarm, but it was too late.

The *Hunley*'s lethal sting was a barbed minelike device affixed to a 20-foot-long spar bolted to the sub's bow. The plan was to ram the enemy ship with the spar, thus inflicting the explosive "torpedo" and then back away, pulling a trigger rope and detonating 135 pounds of black powder from a safe distance.

Amid a hail of small-arms fire unleashed by the *Housatonic*'s crew, the *Hunley* rammed her spar into the ship's vulnerable wooden side and backed away. Two minutes later, the torpedo cord was pulled, and a massive explosion tore the aft quarter out of the *Housatonic*. She sank in minutes—but in relatively shallow water with the loss of only five Yankee lives.

Then, the *Hunley* disappeared. She was seen signaling with a dim blue light to observers waiting on Sullivan's Island that she was now returning home, but she never arrived. That mysterious blue signal light offered the only proof the *Hunley* had survived the blast that sent the *Housatonic* to the sea floor. The *Hunley* had met with success and changed history, but the journey she undertook on that day would last 131 years.

The mystery of her disappearance lingered for many decades. Where did she go down? Was she disabled somehow during her encounter with the *Housatonic*? Did she collide with another vessel? Was her loss due to human or mechanical failure? No one knew.

Finding the lost *Hunley* was the quest of generations of divers. Historians always believed she would be found somewhere on the sea floor between the spot where the *Housatonic* sank and the safety of shore. In May 1995 adventure-novelist Clive Cussler led a group of shipwreck hunters in search of the answers. The object Cussler's team found (and which later proved to be the *Hunley*) was buried under 3 feet of silt nearly a thousand feet seaward of the *Housatonic*'s watery grave. It took five years of study, planning, fund-raising, underwater archaeology, and legal wrangling to finally bring her to the surface.

Finally, in August 2000 she was raised in a cradle of steel beams and padding that distributed her weight evenly. She was handled like an enormous, fragile egg. Time had coated her in a thick crust of corroding iron, sea minerals, and marine organisms, which acted as a preservative. More amazingly, the sub's interior had apparently filled early on with a fine, dense mud that froze the *Hunley*'s final moments—and her crew—in an archaeological photograph. Skeletonized remains of all eight crew members were found inside the sub, each one still at his assigned post. Intimate objects discovered with their remains gave eloquent testimony to their humanity; a pocket watch with fob, a beard comb, even a "lucky $20 gold piece" from a sweetheart back home.

The *Hunley* now rests in a temporary research laboratory, the Warren Lash Conservation Center, in North Charleston where, slowly, her secrets are surrendering to forensic study and state-of-the-art preservation science. Someday Lieutenant Dixon and his crew of seven brave men will receive the dignified military funeral and burial they were denied in 1864, and the *Hunley* will rest in a maritime museum worthy of her place in maritime history. It was a long journey—136 years in all—but at last the *Hunley* came home.

A Potpourri of South Carolina Facts

• South Carolina has a total area of 31,113 square miles.

• According to the 2000 census, the population of South Carolina is about four million.

• On May 23, 1788, South Carolina became the eighth state to ratify the Constitution.

• South Carolina has forty-six counties.

• Horry County is the largest county east of the Mississippi River, covering 1,133 square miles.

• According to the 2000 census, Greenville County has the largest population, at 379,616.

• The highest point is Sassafras Mountain, 3,560 feet above sea level; the lowest point is sea level at the Atlantic Ocean.

• South Carolina has 187 miles of coastline.

• The Edisto River is the longest black-water river in the world.

• South Carolina's state nickname is the Palmetto State, for the state tree.

• Columbia is the state capital and largest city, with a population of 116,278 according to the 2000 census.

• The state bird is the Carolina wren.

• The state flower is the yellow jessamine.

• The state animal is the white-tailed deer.

• The state dog is the Boykin spaniel.

• The state wild-game bird is the wild turkey.

• The state reptile is the loggerhead turtle.

• The state fish is the striped bass.

• The state insect is the praying mantis.

• The state fruit is the peach.

• The state shell is the lettered olive.

• The state stone is blue granite.

• The state gemstone is amethyst.

• The state beverage is milk.

• The state dance is "the Shag."

• The state mottoes are *dum spiro, spero* which means "While

I breathe, I hope," and *Animis opibusque parati*, "Prepared in mind and resources."

• The state song is "Carolina," with words from a poem by Henry Timrod and set to music by Anne Custis Burgess.

• The major industries of the state are textiles and tourism.

• The principal farm products are vegetables, cotton, peaches, and tobacco.

• More Revolutionary War battles and skirmishes were fought in South Carolina than in any other state—more than 200.

• South Carolina was the first state to pass the Ordinance of Secession and secede from the Union on December 20, 1860.

• The town of Abbeville is known as "the birthplace and deathbed of the Confederacy."

Bibliography

And Hugo was his name: Hurricane Hugo, a diary of destruction, September 21, 1989. Sun City West, Ariz.: C. F. Boone Publishing Co., 1989.

Bacot, D. Huger. "Jonathan Lucas and Rice Culture." *South Carolina Historical Magazine,* November 1953.

Bodie, Idella. *South Carolina Women,* rev. and exp. ed. Orangeburg, S.C.: Sandlapper Publishing, Inc., 1991.

Bolick, Julian Stevenson. *Georgetown Ghosts including the Gray Man of Pawley Island and other ghosts of Waccamaw Neck.* Clinton, S.C.: Jacob Brothers, 1956.

Chesnut, Mary Boykin. *A Diary from Dixie.* Edited by Ben Ames Williams. Cambridge, Mass.: Harvard University Press, 1980.

Credico, Mary A. *Mary Boykin Chesnut: A Confederate Woman's Life.* Madison, Wis.: Madison House Publishers, Inc., 1996.

Edgar, Walter. *South Carolina: A History.* Columbia, S.C.: University of South Carolina Press, 1998.

Edwards, Lillie J. *Denmark Vesey.* New York: Chelsea House Publishers, 1990.

Fraser, Walter J. *Charleston! Charleston! The History of a Southern City*. Columbia, S.C.: University of South Carolina Press, 1989.

Hamer, Fritz. "Barbecue, Farming and Friendship: German Prisoners of War and South Carolinians, 1943–46," *Proceedings of the South Carolina Historical Association* 1994: 61–74.

Hill, Barbara Lynch. *Summerville: A Sesquicentennial Edition of the History of The Flower Town in the Pines*. West Columbia, S.C.: Wentworth Printing, 1998.

Huntsinger, Elizabeth Robertson. *Ghosts of Georgetown*. Winston-Salem, N.C.: John F. Blair, 1995.

Jones, Lewis P. *South Carolina, A Synoptic History for Laymen*. Orangeburg, S.C.: Sandlapper Publishing, Inc., 1971.

Kwist, Margaret Scott. *Porch Rocker Recollections of Summerville, S.C.* Summerville, S.C.: Linwood Press, Inc., 1980.

Lachicotte, Alberta Morel. *Georgetown Rice Plantations*. Georgetown, S.C.: Georgetown County Historical Society, 1993.

Leland, John. *Stede Bonnet: "Gentleman Pirate" of the Carolina Coast*. Charleston, S.C.: Charleston Reproductions, 1972.

Lipscomb, Terry W. *South Carolina in 1791: George Washington's Southern Tour*. Columbia, S.C.: South Carolina Department of Archives and History, 1993.

Marion, John Francis. *The Charleston Story*. Harrisburg, Pa.: Stackpole Books, 1978.

Miller, Edward A., Jr. *Gullah Statesman: Robert Smalls from Slavery to Congress 1839-1915.* Columbia, S.C.: University of South Carolina Press, 1995.

Moore, John Hammond. "Nazi Troopers in South Carolina, 1944–46." *South Carolina Historical Magazine,* October 1980.

Pittman, Clyde Calhoun. *Death of a Gold Mine.* Columbia, S.C.: R. L. Bryan Company, 1972.

Price, Charles, and George C. Rogers. *The Carolina Lowcountry, Birthplace of American Golf, 1786.* Hilton Head Island, S.C.: Sea Pines Co., 1980.

Ripley, Warren. *Charles Towne, Birth of a City.* Charleston, S.C.: The Evening Post Publishing Co., 1970.

Roberts, Nancy. *Blackbeard and Other Pirates of the Atlantic Coast.* Winston-Salem, N.C.: J. F. Blair, 1993.

————. *Ghosts of the Carolinas.* Columbia, S.C.: University of South Carolina Press, 1988.

Robertson, David. *Denmark Vesey: The Buried History of America's Largest Slave Rebellion and the Man Who Led It.* New York: Alfred A. Knopf, 1999.

Rogers, George C., Jr. *The History of Georgetown County, South Carolina.* Columbia, S.C.: University of South Carolina Press, 1970.

Rogers, George C., and C. James Taylor. *A South Carolina Chronology, 1497–1992.* 2d ed. Columbia, S.C.: University of South Carolina Press, 1994.

Rosen, Robert. *A Short History of Charleston.* 2d ed. Columbia, S.C.: University of South Carolina Press, 1982.

Steedman, Marguerite C. *The South Carolina Colony.* New York: Crowell-Collier Press, Macmillean, 1970.

Stockton, Robert P. *The Great Shock: The Effects of the 1886 Earthquake on the Built Environment of Charleston, South Carolina.* Easley, S.C.: Southern Historical Press, Inc., 1986.

Usner, Daniel H., Jr. "Rebeckah Lee's Plea on 'Fetching of Drink for an Indian Squaw,' " 1684. *South Carolina Historical Society Magazine,* October 1984.

Uya, Okon Edet. *From Servitude to Service: Robert Smalls, 1839–1915.* Ph.D. diss., University of Wisconsin, 1969.

Walker, Lois. "The History of the Haile Gold Mine," *Carologue* 15, no. 2: (summer 1999): 8–13.

Waring, Joseph I., M.D. *The First Voyage and Settlement at Charles Town 1670–1680.* Columbia, S.C.: University of South Carolina Press, 1970.

Index

About the Authors

J. Michael McLaughlin

J. Michael McLaughlin has been living in and writing about the Lowcountry for more than twenty years. During that time his interests in history, architecture, and the legendary Charleston lifestyle have led him into countless adventures.

His writing has found its way into numerous regional and national magazines such as *Modern Maturity* and *Diversion*. His freelance work as an advertising and public-relations consultant has captured national marketing awards. In 1992 he was one of the originators of *Insiders' Guide to Greater Charleston*, an in-depth and comprehensive introduction written for visitors to his favorite Southern city. Incredibly, time and appreciative readers have resulted in eight additional updates now sold nationwide through The Globe Pequot Press.

Michael was raised on a farm in Indiana, but he's quick to point out it was in *southern* Indiana, and "in Charleston, that makes a big difference." He graduated from Indiana University in 1967 with a B.S. degree in business-journalism, aiming for a Madison Avenue career in advertising. Instead, his first writing job turned out to be in Vietnam, where, as a war correspondent, he won a Bronze Star (exceptional meritorious achievement) for his coverage of the 101st Airborne Division during the ill-fated 1968 Tet Offensive.

After a decade back home in Indiana as an award-winning writer-producer for several Midwestern ad agencies, he joined the writers' colony in Key West, Florida. And that's where he was living when 1979's Hurricane David forced him to evacuate the island and he discovered Charleston. Ever since, he has enjoyed writing about South Carolina and the Lowcountry's charming, if idiosyncratic, ways.

Lee Davis Todman

Native South Carolinian Lee Davis Todman was raised in Charleston and returned to her beloved city in 1987 after pursuing her education and nine-year stint away in "the urban fast lane." Lee received a journalism degree from the University of Georgia in 1976 and did graduate work there in public relations. In 1979 she began her career in Atlanta, working for several ad agencies, among them J. Walter Thompson USA, where she was a senior media planner.

The pull of the ocean and the traditions of her childhood proved too strong to abandon for long, though: "Who says you can't go home again?" Since returning, Lee has worked as a freelance advertising and marketing consultant on local and regional accounts, creating and implementing many award-winning campaigns. In 1997 she joined Mike as coauthor of *Insiders' Guide to Charleston* and was instrumental in bringing about six more editions of this best-selling city guide. She has collaborated with Mike on articles for national magazines as well as numerous business presentations.

Succumbing to the allure of the Historic District, Lee has undertaken the renovation of an old house (ca. 1803) in the downtown peninsula area. Although it has proved to be both a test of her endurance and a labor of love, it provides a perfect setting from which to ponder the timeless beauty and vitality of South Carolina.